BETTER

GR**A**DES
IN COLLEGE

WITH LESS EFFORT

By Kenneth A. Green

BARRON'S

BARRON'S EDUCATIONAL SERIES, INC.
Woodbury, New York • London • Toronto

BARRON'S EDUCATIONAL SERIES, INC.
113 Crossways Park Drive
Woodbury, New York 11797

Library of Congress Catalog Card No. 70–134238

International Standard Book Number 0–8120–0415–9

PRINTED IN THE UNITED STATES OF AMERICA

345   045   15 14 13 12 11

CONTENTS

4   HOW TO CRAM AND PASS EXAMS   36

5   LIBRARIES, REFERENCES ETC.   47

6   TERM PAPERS, THEMES, REPORTS   56

Contents

Introduction

Now you can learn how to play the college system (and win) the easy way. The experience and shortcuts to better grades of recent college grads are spelled out in this book.

The approach is frank, detailed and to-the-point. There is no moralizing on the place and value of grades in higher education — they are merely dealt with as a fact of college life.

If you had to go through high school again it would be much easier the second time around — partly because you'd know what you're up against and how to deal with it. This book gives you the experience, know-how and confidence to deal with college as if you've already been through it.

Why learn how to survive in college the hard way — by painful trial and error. With this book near at hand, or better yet distilled to its basic precepts and committed to memory, and practiced, you should have little trouble making better grades in college with less effort.

CHAPTER **I**

Better Grades with Less Effort

Is there really a way to get better college grades with *less effort?* Yes, there most surely is. And it's a legitimate way, too. We'll tell you about it—from first-hand experience.

Because of the stiff competition you're up against in college, it is important that you—a serious student—arm yourself with as many legitimate devices as you can find to help you get the very best return from your college effort. This book offers such devices.

Beating the college system

This book might well be entitled "Instant Experience." There was a temptation to use a title inadvertently suggested by a college dean who reviewed the manuscript. Somewhat dismayed by its contents, he called it a book on "How to Beat the College System."

That's a flattering title, but it's also a little shady. "How to Survive the College System without Killing Yourself" might be more appropriate.

This book simply offers practical shortcuts to help you get that degree with less sweat—to help you save time and strain and still improve your grades. It tells you how more than a dozen recent college graduates would go through college if they had it to do all over again. At this point, you may suspect this study guide is unusual. It is. Most study guides are written by education specialists—teachers, deans, psychologists and others whose lives are academically oriented. These education specialists may have something to offer. But let's face it: They are people who are naturally academic—so much so that they make education, teaching or counseling their careers.

We think they are further removed than we are from the contemporary college student and his problems. They view things from a different perspective, and there are certain "fine points" and shortcuts that they would not tell you.

We've been there—recently

Once in a while you'll run across a study guide written by some fatherly old professor who starts out with something like this:

"Boys and girls, you are setting sail on a fantastic and wondrous journey across the Sea of Knowledge. You will see and learn many things. Work hard, apply yourself and learn all you can, for you will be building a foundation to enrich your lives . . ."

We young smart alecks don't mean to mock the kindly old gentlemen who take this approach, but such an opening is hardly attuned to a high-pressure education system where freshmen start fielding 10-letter words, higher mathematics, tough instructors and back-breaking work loads from their first week on.

Most study guides advise against cramming. We not only advocate cramming—we tell you how to do it.

Neither the author nor those whose experiences fill these pages are specialists in the field of education—with two noteworthy exceptions at the end of this book. But we have plenty to offer. As college graduates with recent college experience, we face our subject not as statisticians and professional educators, but as young people who have recently stood where you are now standing.

Our experience is your gain

We made it to graduation—somehow. For a rare few, getting a degree was nothing spectacular. It was just a matter of spending four years working in some loosely defined direction. For most of us, however, it wasn't a darned bit easy. Making it through college was a back-breaker. We didn't have a 40-hour work week and a nine-to-five routine with weekends free. *But maybe we could have, had we known at the outset certain techniques we had learned by the time we graduated.*

We—those of us whose little bits of wisdom are contained in this book—like to think we're a combination of success stories. But we'd probably break our own arms patting ourselves on our hindsides. Besides, you're buying this book to find out how *you* can get better grades with less effort.

The experiences of others who have recently tromped through college can help you by showing better ways to cope with college and how to avoid some of the common pitfalls.

How this book developed

We got together as friends shortly after graduating from our respective colleges and universities. As we began to swap stories and rehash our college careers, it became evident to everyone that college could have been a lot easier and more enjoyable.

As we discussed the techniques each of us had discovered, developed, or learned the hard way, we realized we had covered a virtual gold mine of information. Such comments as: "Maybe if I had done what you did, English Lit would have been a lot easier," flew back and forth.

One participant remarked toward the end of the evening, "I think if I'd heard this discussion about five years ago, my whole college experience would have been different." Someone suggested writing down our ideas on paper and another, turning to this author, said: "You're a writer. Why don't you tie all this together in the form of a book?"

Thus began months of work. We got together several more times and new faces joined the group, bringing still new ideas.

Finally our ideas were combined into a pamphlet and we sent mimeographed copies to friends on several campuses, asking them for frank evaluations. The results were gratifying.

Every student offered praise and many offered ideas of their own. The criticisms and suggestions were evaluated, and those which had merit have been implemented into the final version.

The professionals agreed

We took the manuscript to some educators at nearby colleges and asked for their opinions. Most thought the material a little unorthodox, but they agreed it was very practical.

The dean of students at one college admitted frankly: "You've outlined procedures that no dean could ever prescribe for his students. YOUR MANUSCRIPT IS SOUND, BUT IT SEEMS TO TELL THE READER HOW TO BEAT THE COLLEGE SYSTEM."

We were flattered by the comment, yet we almost expected it. Because, in a way, this book does outline a way to beat the college system . . . not in a devious, underhanded way, but in a simple head-on way.

Two very prominent educators were so impressed that they offered material of their own to go with our work. One is a professor of law who has taught at several top-notch institutions. The other is a professor of political science and a counselor. Their joint contribution constitutes a later chapter.

The aim of this book, as you probably have gathered, is to help you, the student, achieve your goal more easily—to help you get that college degree. We believe that a few basic ground rules and some proven techniques for getting good grades will save you a lot of hours, headaches and work.

Simple things—big difference

Unfortunately, there is no formula for getting a college degree by merely spending four years in class and snapping your fingers. But there are hundreds of ways to make better use of your effort. Unlike many study guides, this book will not tell you how much time to spend on each course or how to budget your time or even how to live your college life. Instead, it will tell you how to do the *simple things* which make a *big dif-*

ference in college and how several successful college graduates managed to find easier ways to get that degree.

You need not possess a gifted intellect in order to get a degree, so long as you have the desire to do well. You have the ability to graduate right now. If you were not considered capable of making it through college, you would not have been admitted.

Despite an individual's potential and his willingness to work, he is not guaranteed success in college. Many students are not making the grade these days simply because their study efforts are not paying off.

Perhaps you feel you are an overworked "average" student. You probably worry about your grades and a handful of other problems and you wonder if you'll ever make it through your institution.

We know exactly what you're going through. We know firsthand the worries connected with getting admitted to advanced courses. We know what it feels like to study the wrong material when preparing for an exam. We've all experienced quarters or semesters when each instructor acts as though his course is the only one you're taking. And, we've all known the bitter frustration of knocking ourselves out to get a good grade—and ending up with a lousy one.

Save time and work less

Now that we've sized up the situation, let's get down to business. We truly believe that if you carefully consider the tips outlined and use a portion of that gray matter, you will profit time-wise and grade-wise. Students whose grades are marginal, those who are not making the grades they should be making and those who are getting good grades but have little leisure, should find several shortcuts in this study guide. *Because we learned by experience that there are ways to make better grades with less effort.*

CHAPTER 2

Jump into That Classroom

From the day a student starts college until the moment he picks up his degree and walks out of the halls of ivy, he is a multi-digit number on a registration card. He is but one of hundreds or thousands of students—a little bundle of anonymity who clutches his books and trots from classroom to classroom amidst a sea of other little bundles clutching their books. He has a name that's listed in each course roster in the traditional, alphabetized "last-name-first, first-name, middle-name-last" fashion. He is simply "another student."

From the word *go*, the biggest favor a student can do for himself is to become a *person*—someone whose academic interests, problems and future really matter.

Who's who?

So when you get started in each course, *get to know your instructor*. In the larger classes, most students fail to become known by face and name. It is, understandably, hard to make a personal contact in a huge class where an instructor may show an air of indifference toward the many faces absorbing his lecture. Yet, you will notice there will always be a small handful of students gathered around the lecture podium before or after class talking with the instructor. Join them. Making yourself known, by name, is one of the quickest techniques you can use to reinforce your study effort and to get good grades.

Some instructors announce office hours during which they invite students to come in to talk with them. If your instructors have these office hours, take advantage of their time. If they don't, then make an occasional contact before or after class or by appointment.

Get advice—it's free

Instructors can give you valuable advice about their courses and often about others. And, if you're having difficulty with a course or are striving for a top grade, you'll find that an instructor will be more concerned with a grade given to you—*a person with a name*—than he would be with just an alphabetized name or a seat number in his grading book. See him when you first hit a rough spot. Don't wait until two or three days before a test or final exam to run for help. You cannot expect any instructor to be interested in your academic problems or to show much sympathy or concern if you wait until the end of a course to approach him for advice.

You've got to see him, talk with him, and solicit his suggestions the moment you sense you're in for a difficult time.

Always be courteous in your dealings with instructors and don't overdo the apple-polishing routine. Some instructors may buy the apple business, but most won't.

Shyness pays no dividends

Never be afraid to ask an instructor questions. No matter how shy you are—or how aloof and even icy-eyed an instructor appears to be—ask questions when you want information.

In a sense, this idea of asking questions is one of the important themes of this somewhat unusual study guide. All contributors stressed the idea of asking questions. You are in college to *learn,* and in order to learn, you have to ask questions.

Making a personal contact with your instructors, becoming known to them by name and asking them appropriate questions are the ways by which you, the student, can rise out of that sea of anonymity.

Getting lost?

So ask questions. If you get confused during a lecture, get your hand into the air and ask for a clarification. Instructors are there to teach you a given subject, and they are paid to do this. Sometimes, because of their high degree of familiarity with a subject, instructors will leave their students behind during lectures. But most instructors are courteous enough to clarify a point that a student doesn't understand. Instructors will have a higher regard for those students who make a special effort to understand the subject. And when you ask for an elaboration or clarification, you reduce the chances of becoming more confused as the lecture or course progresses.

Some instructors may set ground rules about asking questions. In large classes, they may ask that students save questions until the end of the lecture or after class. If an instructor specifically spells this out, then respect his rules. But if he does not set such a ground rule, then ask your question during the lecture.

Let the sheep stare

You might be embarrassed to raise your hand and ask a question. Well, don't be. If you find that you are confused or are getting lost during a lecture, it is probable that other students are in the same boat but don't have the initiative or courage to raise their hands. Sometimes it is very hard for a student, particularly in a large class, to raise his hand suddenly and perhaps draw icy or amused glances from others because he is interrupting the proceedings. But go ahead. Raise your hand. You're paying your fees, aren't you? You're there to learn, aren't you? Be a pioneer if you must. It is probable that once you've "broken the ice," others who are puzzled will follow.

If you just cannot make yourself ask questions during a lecture, try asking your question after class or at some other time, such as immediately before the next lecture in the same course.

The effort pays

Instructors will recognize your effort to understand a course. Chances are that it will pay off when grades are handed out, too. For example, if you have to approach an instructor frequently for additional explanation, your face will become known to him. Make sure he knows your name. If he doesn't, let him know it. Tell him who you are and ask for an explanation. Few humane instructors will flunk an undergraduate student who really appears to be trying, unless the student simply cannot grasp the course.

And asking applies not only to lecture material, but also to outside assignments and reading material which is not clear to you. Here's another thing to remember: Most instructors teach a course because they like to teach and because they like their subject. They have to like both to lecture day after day. In fact, once you've asked your question, you may actually find it is hard to turn them off.

Test? What test!

If an examination is approaching and your instructor has not briefed the class on what to expect, ask him about it. Some instructors will never say a word about a test—other than that it is coming—until someone in class asks. Then, when they're asked, many will practically give away the questions or at least a very good indication of what to study.

This idea of asking can't be overemphasized. No one will help you unless you help yourself. Of course, a student should not be a chronic and irritating question-asker. Anything can be carried to extremes. It would be unwise, for example, to ask questions that would have been answered if you had read your assigned material. And it might be antagonizing to ask too many questions too often during lectures day after day. But applied sensibly when needed, this idea of asking questions can pay off.

Seek a re-phrasing

It can also pay off during exams. Suppose you get a question you simply do not understand on an exam. Trot up to the instructor or proctor and tell him you don't understand it. Don't go scribbling off with a bunch of knowledge that may not apply to the question. If you are not able to interpret the question, you can get on the wrong course with your answer and your effort may be a total waste. Instructors are usually willing to rephrase any "thinking" type of question. In fact, in his rephrasing, he may give you a few tips about what he's looking for in an answer. This is a fairly common occurrence.

A slip of the lip

Now—here's some advice which *must be used cautiously* on thinking type or interpretive test questions: If you *do* understand a question and don't know the answer, but think that a hint or two might give you something to work with in formulating an answer, go on up and ask your instructor to paraphrase the question. Be careful here. Don't ask for a rephrasing of a simple question that requires a simple and obvious answer—the kind you either know or don't know. Use it only for the complicated essay-type questions.

The author is not suggesting that you try to squeeze information out of your instructor. Absolutely not! But if your instructor is willing to discuss a question a little bit and could give you, shall we say, some new "insights". . . . (Enough said.)

Just to hear him is not to know him

Part of this idea of getting to know your instructor includes getting to know something about him. If you have, say, six courses with six different instructors, it will help to find out something about the ones who teach the rougher courses. Try to talk with good students who have taken the same or other courses from your instructors.

Get several viewpoints

Speak to more than one student, so that you get a broader viewpoint. These students can give you an idea of what points in a course demand the most attention and the kind of examinations you can expect. When preparing for tests, it can be very helpful to know in advance whether an instructor employs short-answer memorization questions or those requiring detailed or computation answers. By talking with these other students you'll also find out whether an instructor looks for specific details or accepts generalizations.

Learning a little about your instructor helps not only in studying for exams, but also in taking class notes and reading textbook material.

Again, we emphasize speaking with good students, particularly if you tend to investigate the toughness of an instructor's grading practices before you sign up for his class. Jugheads, goof-offs, and borderline students may have axes to grind and their evaluations might well reflect their own academic inabilities.

Before you pass by an instructor merely because an acquaintance warned you with "that so-and-so flunked me in calculus," find out how many other courses your acquaintance has flunked. In other words, temper the evaluation with your own knowledge of the advising student.

Can you get old tests?

If you have a chance to see examination questions given in a particular course, use them to determine the type of questions you can expect. But don't lean *too heavily* on exams given previously. Textbooks and teaching syllabuses frequently change, and instructors do not always give the same test questions from one semester to the next. (Some vary their questions intentionally, knowing many students like to make use of old tests.) And, of course, different instructors teaching the same course will probably give different tests.

Old tests given by the same instructor in a different course at the same level of sophistication as one you're taking can help you determine the basic format of his examinations—even though the subject matter is not identical.

The chief advantages in looking at old tests lie in (1) your ability to anticipate and prepare for a general line or type of questions that may be asked on your test, and (2) spotting subject matter you're expected to know.

Some profs develop habits

Often, through old tests given in earlier semesters and from remarks passed along by a professor's former students, you can spot a specific subject or area favored in examinations. Some professors are buggy about particular phases of a course or about some segment within their whole field.

For example, one contributor noted he had a literature professor who was a "nut" about three early American authors. In most courses the professor taught—from the freshman level up—he found some way of including at least one book by one of these authors in the course material—and threw in a heavily-weighted final exam question involving the author or book. Naturally, a lit major would catch on after two courses. But the student casually taking a general literature survey course or some elective lit course on a one-shot basis under this professor might not know about this practice or realize he could expect such a question—unless he did a little research.

What's your specialty, doctor?

Some professors whose doctorate research was in an area which they cover in their courses delight in repeatedly testing in that area to see how their students respond—and to check their knowledge, understanding, analysis and observations of the favored topic.

The more you can find out about your professor and his "pet subjects," the better prepared you'll be to anticipate his exam questions.

In fact, some students automatically make it a habit to find out the points on which their instructors are authorities.

To make a simple analogy, suppose you're an authority on baseball and you're teaching your son about sports. If you were to ask him questions to determine how much he'd learned from you, you'd be especially interested in knowing what he could tell you about baseball, wouldn't you?

Was I that bad?

After taking an examination, you may be distressed to find your grade is less than you think you honestly deserved. It could pay you to consult the instructor *if you approach the matter carefully and tactfully.* If the paper was marked by a grader or assistant, you might appeal directly to your instructor. Be careful not to criticize the grader.

If your instructor graded the papers himself and you think yours was not properly evaluated or that a grading error was made, you might approach your instructor, paper in hand, and ask if he has a moment to go over it with you *to help you understand where you got off the track.* Approach it on that basis: You erred on your test and would be grateful for his help in showing you where you fell down or how you could have improved it. If he's not willing, then forget it and don't argue.

A grading error or oversight, if one was made, will show up when he goes over your paper with you. And he will be the one to "discover" the error—not you. This indirect approach keeps the instructor in the role of a teacher, and does not put him on the defensive.

Never defend a fool

If there is a rare occasion where you wish to defend the merits of an answer during the post-test review, be gentle and cautious and *accept his rebuttal graciously.* Never suggest to your instructor that he missed the point of your answer. (If he did, it's probably your fault anyway and you must expect to pay some penalty for not expressing yourself clearly.)

Any defense you offer on your interpretation or point of view in answering a subjective exam question will be useless unless it is apparent from the answer that you *know the material*. Therefore, never try to con your way into extra points if you bluffed in the first place. In explaining why you answered the question as you did, stick to the "How could I have done a better job?" approach.

Don't seek a post-test review if you were unprepared for the examination—lest your question, "How could I have done a better job?" be answered with, "By reading the assigned material."

We offer more don't's than do's in this area of getting a post-test review because so much depends upon the individual instructor and your own personality. Common sense, your knowledge of the instructor and the nature of your own personality should be your guide in this whole matter.

Keep in mind that any time you're granted an audience with your instructor, he is doing you a favor or at least is doing more than his job requires. No matter how much tuition you're paying, your instructor does not owe you a private conference or post-test review.

Two other don't's: Never say "You made a mistake in grading my paper" or "I think you are wrong." No one likes to be told he's wrong—especially a college instructor when he's challenged by a student. Students who assume the role of an auditor placing the instructor on the defensive will only create unnecessary friction. Remember that it is the instructor who hands out your final grade—right or wrong.

When to seek a post-mortem

Be conservative about running up for a review of your test. Do it only when you need help in understanding your errors and when it might materially help your grade.

One student, for example, said he received a C+ in a course after carrying a strong B into the final examination. He was baffled, and using the gentle "where did I goof?" approach, asked his instructor what had happened. The instructor hauled out the student's final examination paper and reviewed it with the student. During the review, the teacher realized the student had merely taken an unusual approach in writing a 30-point answer. The student walked out with a final course grade of B.

Keep in mind that any time you request an instructional review of your exam, you're actually gambling. You're subjecting your product—the examination paper—to further scrutiny. An instructor is as likely to err in your favor as he is to undergrade. If it becomes apparent to him in re-reading your test that he (or a grading assistant) over-graded your paper, he might well knock it down a few points.

A request for an instructional review is simply that; it is not a request for favors. You may get a favor, but don't expect it. If you received a better grade than you deserved, don't gamble for more and maybe lose.

Nearly everyone cuts a class

It is easy for this author to sit back and preach, "Don't cut classes." But it must be said. Cutting leaves a lousy impression on instructors and it leaves you short of lecture information—notes and material you'll need when preparing for tests.

The academicians who write study guides that are full of platitudes will merely tell students not to cut classes. And they let it go at that. We don't say that you simply must never, never cut a class. It is a very rare student who goes through four years of college without a cut, or maybe even five or 10 or more cuts. Some students pick up five or six cuts in just one day—such as the day before vacation when they leave early to hit the slopes or go home.

So maybe you'll have occasions when you want to cut a class or two. If you have a *good* excuse for a cut and your instructor takes attendance, it would be wise to give him your excuse. Some instructors treat students like children and set a limit on the number of cuts allowed.

Some cut their own throats

Many students have actually flunked courses simply because they exceeded the two or three cuts allowed by the instructor.

Maybe this *is* unfair. If a student passes his tests and does his work on time, it seems reasonable that he should pass the course. But some instructors don't reason this way. They believe a student should attend so many lectures in order to pass the course. Maybe it seems unfair, but it is an instructor's prerogative to make the ground rules.

Say you're sorry

If you take a cut here or there, get hold of someone in your class and copy his notes immediately. Don't wait for several weeks, or you probably will forget. If you wait until shortly before an exam, you may find that your classmates need their notes to study and won't lend them to you. Then the lecture material will be gone forever. When you borrow notes, make sure they are good. If they're fragmentary or illegible, borrow someone else's.

Naturally, the best advice is: Do Not Cut. Surveys have shown that the students with better college grades take fewer cuts, and that the poorest students have the highest rate of cutting.

The class is not a bedroom

And when you do attend class, we advise against sleeping or studying material for other courses. If you do sleep or study other material, don't get caught.

Any instructor is entitled to be irritated when he sees students goofing off, sleeping or studying during his lecture. When final grades are handed out, you can hardly expect any benefit of doubt if you made a habit of these pursuits.

Hearing and listening—a difference

When you are in class, pay attention. *Listen* to the lecture—don't merely *hear* it. Hearing a lecture takes little work. But sometimes it takes real effort to listen. Listening means paying attention and absorbing what is said. Sometimes it is downright hard to force yourself to listen to a boring lecture or monotone instructor. Besides, everyone has a tendency to day-dream occasionally.

Love-life versus lecture

Try to avoid preoccupations and forget your personal life, the forthcoming weekend, your problems and whatever else tries to compete for your attention during a class—even if the lecture material is uninspiring. In other words, don't goof off. Look at it this way: You have to sit there anyway, so pay attention and force yourself to *listen*. If you don't, you may miss important points and your test grades will suffer.

Move up

If your seat is way in the back of the class and you have trouble paying attention, hearing or seeing, move forward. Sometimes hearing and eyesight difficulties can partially account for a student's lack of interest or a tendency to goof off during class. Instructors are pretty sympathetic about this type of problem, and if seats are assigned, they'll usually approve a change.

The late teens and early to middle 20's are times when hearing or eyesight difficulties are apt to show up. If you think you have a hearing problem, see a physician or specialist. The same goes for your eyesight. Often, students will develop trouble reading, studying, and paying attention in class because of an eyesight problem that develops gradually during college. And because the problem may creep in over a period of years, people often are not really aware of it.

Glasses in classes

Sometimes persons who develop vision problems will have frequent headaches or restlessness, but these give-away symptoms don't always appear. If you even suspect your vision is not up to snuff, have your eyes checked.

One graduate contributor, who began developing studying problems during his junior year, got suspicious and had his eyes checked. A specialist put glasses on the student's face and everything beyond 30 feet suddenly came back into focus. His study efficiency picked up markedly.

People frequently are reluctant to admit they have an eyesight problem and have to wear glasses. Contact lenses can be expensive, and there's the old saying about lasses in glasses. One contributor suggested this alternate phrase: She passes classes who puts on her glasses.

Now that we've started into the subject of physical problems, we get to the realm of sickness.

Attitudes vary

Instructors can be far apart in their attitudes toward illness.

Some are very sympathetic and will forgive a student for cuts and missed tests without a trace of skepticism. Headaches, colds, toothaches—anything that comes along is an adequate excuse. Then there are those who seemingly refuse to recognize illness as an excuse and who demand attendance and production despite little maladies. Some may nearly demand a notarized statement from a hospital attesting to a student's illness. These "tough" instructors may well be ones who—somewhere along the line—felt they were played for saps by chronic malingerers.

Students who go overboard on the "sickness" routine are going to pay for it. Instructors are not dummies. Most can spot the phonies pretty quickly.

Get the problem on record

Students who have a prolonged or recurring illness should consult a physician or practitioner who will inform a school official or dean. And students who are unable to show up for a test or lab or who fail to meet some other academic demand because of their own or a family illness should telephone someone in the department or division—even a secretary—*in advance* of the absence. If this is impossible, the student should be able to document his illness claim with a note from a physician or someone else whose statement will be accepted. Unless an instructor is very liberal in his views toward illness as an excuse or has a firm knowledge of the student, he cannot be expected to be sympathetic toward a student who shows up a day or two later offering an illness story as an excuse for missing a test.

Upon returning to class, a student should immediately talk with the instructor to arrange a prompt making up of the work missed.

Taking notes—too many and too few

When you're in class, *listening* to the lecture, you should determine the essential points and write them down. Don't try to write down every word. If you try to write down everything, you may get behind and miss the important stuff. And you'll have just that much more to pore over when you study for tests.

A lot of students, during their college years, have learned that they have been taking too many or too few notes.

Try to understand and absorb the lecture details in your mind. You can generally tell, from the basic lecture presentation, whether your instructor is a nut on details or whether he will want you to understand the main points rather than mimic the little details on a test.

Here again, it can help if you speak with other students who have had the instructor before. Of course, after your first test, you'll be in a better position to judge the amount and type of notes to take. A clue to the type of information you should get down on paper will show up through repetition in the lecture, a repeat of details mentioned in your textbooks and the material an instructor may spend time putting on a blackboard.

Blackboard stuff may serve only to reinforce a verbal point, but you cannot discount the possibility that diagrams, equations and such will be called for in tests.

It seems unfair, but . . .

One contributor had an amusing experience in this regard. During a junior year biology course which touched on organic chemistry, the instructor began discussing the local municipal sewage treatment plant. In a somewhat offhanded manner, he sketched an elaborate diagram showing the step-by-step processes in which sewage was treated, purified and emptied into a river.

Our contributor recalls that a few students feverishly scribbled down the diagram while most of the people—including him—snickered at the seemingly inane activity of the aging instructor. After all, the operations of the treatment plant did not really tie in directly to the theme of the course.

On the final examination, some four months later, lo and behold—for 20 points, "diagram and explain the operations of the local sewage treatment plant."

Our contributor and most of his classmates spent their three hours shooting for a high of 80 per cent.

Take a hint

Some instructors are helpful enough to drop hints during lectures. Obviously, if an instructor announces that a particular point or detail may be called for on a test, it would be smart to get it down in your notes.

If an instructor talks a mile a minute and covers a lot of material rapidly—both broad points and details—you might inquire how much detail he will expect you to remember. This gets back to the theme mentioned earlier: ask questions.

Follow the leader?

Sometimes it is helpful to follow a note-taking pattern of a student next to you *if he is a good student*. But try to be independent, because your neighbor may not be getting down the right type of material. Most contributors advise against this follow-the-leader pattern. Your neighbor just might be one of those types who commit the important stuff to memory as it is spoken and merely write down the supplementary trivia.

Take legible notes in some orderly fashion during your lectures. A scribble of unrelated points may mean something if you read them right after the lecture, but will they several weeks hence, when you're studying for finals? If you have five or six pages of jumbled scratchings in your notebook after each class, it may indicate you take too many notes.

Don't rewrite notes

Here's an important tip: rewriting or typing notes after class is usually a waste of time. Sure, it may make them easier to read later on. Some students believe that rewriting or typing class notes helps them to remember the material. But the advantages may not be worth the extra time involved. You have only so much time available each day and you must devote this time to several courses.

The time required for the mechanical process of rewriting or typing notes would be better spent if you used it for actual studying.

A valuable coffee stain

One educator who holds a doctorate reviewed this book and offered an additional argument against rewriting or typing your class notes:

"Probably the best reason for not rewriting is that you get better recall from original notes." He explained that such things as a coffee stain on the edge of the paper, a dog ear on the page, the abbreviations you used and even a doodle you may have drawn in the margin can trigger a relevant train of thought. In other words, whatever you were thinking about or hearing at the time the doodle, coffee stain (or whatever) was made may come back to your mind when you see the marking later.

One doodle may not be worth a thousand words, but it might be worth a couple—enough to bring back some key ideas.

First impressions

In class, especially at the outset of each course, make a good impression on your instructor. Rather, don't make a bad one!

Every time we meet or observe someone for the first time, we make a quick evaluation of him. We size him up on the basis of what we initially see. Frequently, as all of us have found, time shows that people do not always match our first impression. But somehow, the first impression sticks with us and it takes something dramatic or a long period of time before we can adjust our views.

Hind end Henry

If you come stumbling into class late the first few sessions, fail to get your paperwork handed in on time or maybe blow a quiz or two, you are going to leave a bad first impression. It may take one big pile of convincing to show your instructor you are not really the goof-off he thinks. Maybe you will never be able to erase completely that bad first impression.

Conversely, a good first impression may last longer than you deserve. By creating a good first impression, you may end up with a better grade than you might have gotten otherwise. You may get the benefit of a doubt. Perhaps a final judgment based on a first impression doesn't seem fair. *But it is human nature.*

CHAPTER 3

How to Study

One of the hardest things for most students to do is to settle down and study. People are naturally lazy and are always able to find excuses for not working. People tend to procrastinate and do anything to avoid work.

Many students suddenly find a multitude of other things they feel they should do—at precisely the time they should sit down with the books. There's a letter to write—long overdue, of course—and maybe the room is dirty and should be cleaned. Perhaps some laundry should be dumped into the machine and a couple of "quick" phone calls should be made.

This is how studying *doesn't* get done.

When you sit down to study, do just that: study. If it is just impossible and you can't get down to business, then forget the homework until you *can* settle down. Students who let the irrelevant things bother them, such as the desire for a drink of water, an interesting conversation next door, a messy desk and an unmade bed—will not be able to concentrate properly.

What is concentration?

Many of us admire the people who seem to have an extraordinary ability to concentrate—to throw themselves into something completely. But the ability to concentrate is not a rare mental quality possessed by a few gifted individuals. It is a *doing* thing rather than a *thinking* thing. It is a *decision* to direct the attention to one subject and to ignore unrelated distractions.

We all know someone who can get so absorbed with something—such as a book or newspaper or even a television show —that he won't even hear you speak to him. This is concentration. Concentration really pays off when it comes to studying.

It is easy for an author to say "forget everything else and direct your attention solely to your studying."

But it can be done, and it gets easier with practice. The "rare birds" who are able to concentrate intently are ordinary people who have merely had practice.

Force yourself to forget

So force yourself to forget the trivial distractions and unrelated things when you study. And forget your own little thoughts and daydreams. Push them back out of your mind and force yourself to think only about what you are studying. You'll find you do a better job understanding and remembering if you practice this. And it will get easier as you work at it. You'll find that *one or two hours of concentrated effort will be worth more than several hours of easily distracted, half-hearted study effort.*

So many students can spread out one hour's worth of work over a full evening. And they end up with the feeling that they have really "hit the books" because they spent five hours sitting at the desk.

Don't lose what you have

Some students who have the ability to concentrate when they enter college end up losing it. In high school, they found a quiet place to study at home and developed the ability to concentrate. Upon going to college, they found numerous interesting distractions nearby, such as roommates' chatter, people down the hall, and so on. Don't let this happen. College is more demanding than high school, so if you have the ability to concentrate, try to improve it. Don't lose it.

Do more work in less time

As you develop—or improve—your ability to concentrate, you'll be able to accomplish more work in less time. This will give you additional time to study—and make better grades— or to enjoy some recreational pursuits. Two hours of concentrated study and three hours of recreation will do more for you than five hours of the half-hearted on-again, off-again study effort. You'll accomplish more actual work and you'll get more enjoyment out of the recreation. Neither will interfere with the other.

Worry is waste

Sometimes it is hard to concentrate if you have worries. And if you are worried about your grades—as many students are— that very worry may hurt your grades.

Worry is a mental process which does very little good, tires both the mind and body, and makes concentration difficult. Suppose something is worrying you. Ask yourself, "Is there anything I can do about it right now?"

If your answer is "yes," then do something about it. Get the problem cleared up and out of your mind. If your answer is "no," then try to forget about it until you *can* do something. Don't let the problem plague you. Again, this is more easily said than done, but *try.*

Have you ever noticed how many of the petty little problems that have eaten away at you have somehow gotten straightened out? Somehow, the little ones work themselves out.

One contributor—a man who *seemed* to be totally free of cares—had a strange method of worrying. Every day he took what he called a "five-minute worry break." He'd ponder his problems for a few minutes over his morning coffee, decide when he could do something about each, and then forgot them until he could do something. It sounds corny. But this guy graduated with highest honors and is a pretty happy person. Those of us who knew him know that he had plenty of things to worry about—more than most people.

Be concerned, not worried

Another thought about worrying, as it relates to your academic performance: worry can be a factor in defeat. Psychologists say that *fear of failure* or worries about inadequacies can perpetuate the problem; a person who worries about his performance may—because of the worrying itself—perform poorly. Poor performance causes even greater worry, and the process snowballs straight downhill.

Be concerned, yes—but not worried. Concern is important and it's constructive. Know and understand the difference between the two in your college work.

Keep a record

A common source of worry sometimes pops up when a student suddenly realizes that a test or maybe several are only a few days off. Time has a way of zipping by, and frequently we discover an upcoming deadline we had forgotten. A quick way to avoid being caught unprepared is to make a monthly calendar to log test dates, term paper due dates and other obligations which must be met. The advantage of a monthly log or calendar is that you can see at a glance just what lies ahead for the next month. These calendars, which can be picked up in any bookstore or drawn on a sheet of paper, can help you avoid that sickening "Oh, no, I thought that test was NEXT week" feeling. A calendar will remind you of events you might forget altogether, and will clearly show you the weeks when your time will be jammed with activities. Then you'll be able to plan ahead. It might be smart to list some of your special social or work events on the same calendar so you'll know well in advance where your time will be needed.

The calendar suggestion may sound elementary—even childish. But college is one of the busiest times in a person's life, and it is easy to get fouled up—to goof. Many wise, learned people have made serious and embarrassing goofs by forgetting something—an appointment, social obligation, or other important commitment—merely because they failed to write it down and it got "lost" in a jumble of other things on their minds.

When you're taking several courses, each involving several tests and reports or term papers, and have a pile of social activities or other obligations to remember too, it is very easy (and a common student error) to overlook something . . . or to get into a bind trying to find enough time to prepare adequately for whatever is coming. The calendar is a handy device for avoiding this problem, although it offers no magic for giving you extra time.

Hidden extra time

One way to get extra time, however, is to curb the waste.

Everyone wastes a portion of his time. We spend time going from here to there; we eat, sleep and go about dozens of daily activities. Between these events (and even while doing them) time is wasted. Waiting for a class, a meal, the telephone and a dozen other things takes time from our lives—time that can frequently be put to good use—studying. With a little practice, making use of "wasted" time can become a habit.

Many students feel that in order to study they must get "in the mood." Everything has to be in order and the study material must be carefully laid out on the desk. Studying, to those students, is a project which has a particular time and place in the daily routine. But the smatterings of an idle ten minutes wait here and five minutes there can be put to good use, and these precious minutes really add up.

You need not be an oddball

No one has to be an oddball about this or spend every spare second with his nose in a book. When you know you will have a few minutes of waiting here and there, take a notebook or textbook with you and use it. Glance over a few pages of notes or read a couple of pages in the text. These several momentary exposures to study material will add up in a short while. Even if you have to re-read the material later, you will have had the benefit of a previous exposure. And, the more a student is exposed to his work, the better prepared he will be—not only in his ability to mimic, but in his mind's ability to assimilate the material and make it a part of his thinking.

Making good use of just a portion of your free moments will put you ahead. The hours will rapidly add up, and the time you gain can be used for your own purposes—be it recreation or additional study.

How to read faster

A slow reading rate is one of the *biggest time-wasters* and *one of the most common faults* of college students who have difficulty making good grades. It makes studying a drudgery, wastes valuable time, and causes restlessness, a lack of interest and an inability to concentrate.

Reading specialists say that the faster readers absorb more material—that is, they have a higher comprehension rate—than slower ones. Faster readers are able to concentrate more on the material than the mechanics of moving their eyes from word to word or phrase to phrase and they are less apt to become bored with duller material. One reason they're less likely to become bored is that they pass over the material more rapidly. Compare reading with seeing a movie. Material which could make a good movie is sometimes ruined because the movie is too long. We've all seen movies or plays which were basically good but became dull because the action dragged on or moved too slowly. When it becomes dull, we lose interest and our thoughts may wander.

And so it is with reading. A good novel, or a textbook, may seem very dull to the student who plods through it word by word. That same book may be very interesting or inspiring to the fast reader who can zip through it in a short time. Students who find their college material interesting generally make better grades than those who find it dull. We tend to do best the things we like.

With a little practice, anyone can step up his reading speed and rate of comprehension, no matter how fast he reads now.

Colleges generally offer courses in speed reading. Sometimes a fee is charged and generally the student can plan his speed reading course schedule around his regular classes and other activities. In a speed reading class, students work individually with a mechanical device which can be set to any reading rate and slides over the reading material. The devices virtually force the student to move his eyes over the material more rapidly as the screen slides down the page line by line. And, it covers up the material so that the student cannot go back to re-read previous sentences. Session by session, the speed of the machine is increased.

Increase your own speed—by yourself

It isn't necessary to take a reading course to improve your speed and comprehension rate if you are willing to spend a little time and energy on your own. Here's how you can do it by yourself:

Force yourself to move your eyes over the material just a little faster than you normally do. Start with some light entertainment reading, such as newspapers, magazines or novels. *Keep your eyes moving along the page* just a little faster than normal. At first, you'll probably find this a little uncomfortable because you will think you are missing things. This frustration is natural when you first get started. The first few days, you'll be tempted to regress to your former speed or to go back and re-read something. *But don't do either*. And *don't get discouraged*.

If you have a normal tendency to look at one or two words at a time when you read, try to grasp a couple more with each glance.

Children learning to read look at the individual letters of each word. When they see the word "look," they see each letter. They become aware of an "l" and an "o" and another "o" and then a "k" and finally they determine that the word is "look." As they progress, they become familiar with the combination of letters and finally they recognize the whole word at a glance.

Now, new methods are being formulated and used in the classrooms to improve the teaching of reading.

The mumblers

Students who learned to read through the traditional methods sometimes never get beyond the word-by-word stage of reading. Just as the child goes from the "l" to the "o", some adults go from one or two words to the next one or two words. The prime reason for this is that they *vocalize* when they read. They "say" the words to themselves as they read—either with their lips or in their minds. Millions of literate adults are trapped by their voices, so to speak. They are hung up with a 200 to 300 words a minute reading rate because of vocalization. No, they may not read aloud, and their lips may not even twitch, but they're "saying" the words in their minds as they read. Their reading rate is held to a speaking rate.

The written symbols in the word "look" can be meaningful without being audibly or mentally vocalized. But because we learn to speak before we learn to read, we tend as children to convert the written symbol to something we already know: the spoken word. This conversion may carry through into adult and college life.

Vocalization, whether it is audible (and some adults actually have to read aloud), just a twitch of the lips or a mental "saying" of the word, becomes a habit which is difficult to break. But it can be broken. The way to break it is to catch a couple more words at each glance. Your eyes take in more than one word at a time. Most people with adequate natural or corrected vision see many words at a glance. The slower readers, however, tend to direct their attention to only one or maybe a couple of words at a time.

Try to direct your attention—to catch—a couple more words

at each glance. If you are a vocalizer, you will break the habit. You'll also reduce the amount of muscular motions required of your eyes. Your eyes will be able to jump from phrase to phrase, rather than from word to word. When your eyes are freed from your voice, your reading rate will climb.

Vocalization is helpful if you are trying to memorize something. But you certainly don't want to memorize everything you read.

Keep the eyes moving

As you force yourself to read a couple more words at each glance—*without going back*—in your entertainment reading, you'll find your reading speed increases. Keep working at it. Then, extend your practice to your study material. Move the eyes over the print just a little faster. When you are able to absorb another word or two, use the same system to try for still another word. Eventually, you'll be able to pick out whole phrases at a glance, and within only a couple of weeks (that's about all it takes if you exert yourself a little bit) you'll discover you're absorbing more material at a faster rate and you can catch key ideas at a glance.

On entertainment reading, never go back to re-read. But on class material that you will be tested on, you may have to re-read here and there during the initial reading or at another time.

Some of the really fast readers take in not only a line of print at a time, but often a whole paragraph. Extraordinary reading speeds are not necessary for academic success in college. And unless you have a so-called "photographic memory" and a very high rate of learning, you may not want to tear through books at super speeds.

Skimming and reading

Part of fast reading involves *selective* reading. A complicated mathematics textbook, obviously, is not something to rush through at break-neck speed. It would be slower for anyone to absorb than a novel prescribed for a literature course.

Being selective means paying more attention—and time—to the important points. Skim through the familiar and the simple material, and direct more attention to the essentials.

Underline effectively

When you read textbooks, underline the important points or draw asterisks or vertical lines in the margins. Some students use straight-edges when they underline, and carefully get lined up before they mark the book. This is time consuming and requires extra attention and work. The quickest way is to simply take a pencil or pen and draw a free-hand line under the print. Maybe it isn't as neat as a carefully drawn line, but it is quicker and serves the same purposes. Underlining helps you remember the contents of a sentence, even if you are not aware of it immediately. It also makes the information stand out when you read or scan the material in preparation for a test.

Don't go overboard when you underline or you'll defeat your purpose. If *everything* in your text is important, underline only the *most important* material. You may feel that you'll have to re-read the whole textbook later on. Fine. But the underlining will still serve to point out the core ideas and *most essential* points. If you run short of time and don't have a chance to re-read the whole text, you'll still be able to hit the highlights that you've underlined.

In preparing for an exam, your notes and the underlined points in your textbooks may be sufficient for a good review. You will be very surprised at the amount of supplementary detail *you can recall* when you read underlined material and key sentences.

Marking for emphasis

Occasionally, it is helpful to make notations in the margins of your books. If, on the first reading, it took you quite a while to understand or recognize the importance of a sentence, paragraph or chapter, you might make a condensed note or two in the margin to refresh your memory when you go through the book later. It is also helpful to make a margin note next to material which is emphasized in class or has the earmark of a possible test question.

It's true that underlining in a text reduces its resale value if you try to sell it at the end of the course. Some students are reluctant to underline because it might knock down the trade-in value by a couple of dollars. But those few dollars are barely a drop in the bucket compared to the amount of money and time you're spending just by being in college.

Some students spend a great deal of time writing meticulous notes from their reading material. If you are preparing a term paper or report, or are using a library book which has to go back, it can be helpful to take notes. But it hardly seems worth the time if you're using your own textbook. Underline instead.

The liberty you can take to underline and write in a textbook points out the advantage to *buying* a text rather than borrowing from a friend or from the library.

Underline your class notes when you go over them. This emphasizes the important points so that you can be very selective when you take a quick and final look at the notes before a test.

Memorization made easy

Almost everyone who has had to memorize large quantities of material has devised his own or copied other shortcuts. There are thousands of methods that can be used to speed up or simplify the process of memorization. In fact, several books have been written on the subject of memorization. If you are majoring in a field which will require a large amount of pure memorization during your college career, it might be worth your while to browse through some of these books to get ideas and find shortcuts.

Here's one simple way to speed up memorization of an outline, a series of ideas or a collection of words which must be remembered in an orderly series.

Key words

Find key words in each topic and put them together into some sentence that is easy to remember. This method can be used for even the most sophisticated courses if memorization is required. If you're unable to arrange these key words into some sentence, then use the first letter of each word to make new words and arrange them into a sentence or some little saying—meaningful or not—that you can remember. Sometimes the first letters of each key word will go together to form a meaningless but easily remembered word.

One student used the nonsensical "word" WAAPISAT to remember the proper order of a legal procedure. His key words were WARRANT, ARREST, ARRAIGNMENT, PRELIMINARY, INDICTMENT, SECOND ARRAIGNMENT, TRIAL.

Maybe the letters won't always form an easily pronounced "word," and you'll have to add a vowel or two to make it into something you *can* pronounce. Then remember what letters to discard when you use the word to help you remember something on a test.

Become an author

Here's a sentence a student used to remember the first letters of major words in the Bill of Rights: Four Michigan Students Searched California; Roger Stayed Behind Playing Soccer. His key words, in the proper order, for the Bill of Rights were: Freedoms, Militia, Soldiers, Search, Crimes, Rights, Suits, Bail, People, States.

If you're lucky, key words can be formed into a sentence. Here's one such sentence: "My canopy is frosty and my cowl is flapping closed, I'll mix my rich uncle with his 1900 revolution and I'll blow my nose and run 220 miles home." A pilot who had to be able to go through a lengthy list of memorized procedures very rapidly devised this sentence. It is nonsense, yet all but about five words in the sentence relate to the procedures which must be performed, and they are in the proper order. And, the sentence can be remembered without too much study.

The interference play

Every time you take more than one subject in college, you will encounter a phenomenon called "interference." Interference is an involuntary mental process. It occurs where the learning of one subject tends to interfere with learning another. You may not be conscious of the interference process, but it will always be present to some extent.

The way to reduce the degree of interference you'll experience is to adjust your studying habits so that dissimilar subjects follow each other. When you study courses that are similar but not identical, you will get maximum interference if the subjects are studied one right after another.

When you study several subjects in succession, try to sandwich a completely different course in between two similar courses. Studying a math course in between two similar 'ology' courses, for example, would help reduce interference.

The interference factor also increases when you study for long hours on end. Remember this when you cram. Cramming may have merit, as you'll see in the next chapter, but it does increase the interference.

CHAPTER 4

How to Cram and Pass Exams

"Happy New Year, folks. I've made a New Year resolution. I'm going on the wagon. Let's drink to that . . ."

This is a rather over-worked, annual joke that makes us shudder every time we hear it at a New Year's party.

It's almost as old as another "joke" that is bandied about on campuses at the outset of every new quarter or semester:

"This term is *really* going to be different: I *really* learned a lesson last term and I'm going to blast off and *really* hit the studies this time. No more goofing off. It's gonna be all work this time, REALLY!"

Sure it is. . . .

This "joke" is the most commonly made and broken resolution of college students who didn't quite measure up during the previous term.

The good intention is commendable, but how long does it last? Most students who make resolutions like this are like firecrackers. They start off with a bang. And that's the end of it.

Be realistic

When you feel you've become enlightened, don't set ridiculously rigid study goals and time budgets for yourself—

goals that are obviously impossible to attain. Or you'll soon laugh at their absurdity, break your resolutions and forget all about it.

Many students begin each semester like madmen. They study, study, study like maniacs for two or three weeks, get ahead of their assignment schedules, and then lose their fire.

A test comes along and they scoff, "Phooey. I read that stuff two weeks ago. I'm in fine shape."

This isn't too smart. Research studies in the field of learning and retention say that most forgetting occurs during the first few days after studying something. In other words, most of what you will forget has been forgotten within a week after you've read or studied it. The amount that you will forget in successive weeks is proportionally much less than the amount you forget after the first few days.

As an analogy, let's say you're given a set of 100 facts to learn. And let's say that after three months you will remember only 75 of them—or, expressed differently, you will have forgotten 25 facts. Studies show that the forgotten facts will not have been forgotten in an even proportion during the three month period. Most—say 15 or so—will be forgotten in the first two or three days. The remainder—10—will be forgotten during the next 2 months and 27 days.

Procrastination's only dividend

It's helpful to remember this if you're one of those who does most of his pre-test reading in one surge. If you plan to do *all* the studying for a test in one sitting, it is better to do it the day or evening before a test than a week in advance. If you start off a term like an eager beaver, do it this way: study the material in advance and then *review it* the day or evening before the test.

Traditional study guides will tell you (and we agree) that you should keep up with your reading and studying day by day. But we know that some students don't do it that way; they do it all in one shot, whether it is a week before a test or only a few hours before it.

And now comes one of the most controversial topics in this book: CRAMMING.

Cramming can pay off

The majority of study guides, booklets on academic improvement—call them what you will—say that cramming and burning the midnight oil is of little value and should be highly frowned upon.

We disagree! We feel that cramming and studying into the late-late hours can be *very valuable*. Not one contributor even questioned this! Nor did our reviewing critics.

To support our claims, we point to the findings of the experts: the information about retention. *Most of what you will forget is forgotten during the first few days after learning it*. But if you make that big, hard-hitting study effort (cramming) immediately before an exam, you won't suffer the penalty that comes during the "first few days"—the penalty of a high rate of forgetting. In a sentence, the material you cram is fresh in your mind.

It's now or never

We feel there is another distinct advantage to cramming. When you cram, you're facing a deadline. Unless you're a *very* conscientious student or are studying for a Bar or Ph.D. exam, you're not apt to be too concerned about a test that is, say, three weeks off . . . especially if it is a routine test. But when it is 8 o'clock in the evening and you have a test the next morning, you're apt to feel a little pressure. You're faced with a "now or not at all" situation, and you will be less inclined to goof off or be distracted. You're *concerned*, so you won't mess around.

Finally, cramming is a last resort for getting up to date in your work if you have fallen behind. You shouldn't have fallen behind, but if you did, cramming sessions will give you a chance at least to become exposed to the material that you'll be responsible for knowing on a test. If you failed to learn or study the material as the term progressed, you can't lose much by cramming, except a few hours of sleep. *In most subjects, it is better to be tired and informed than wide awake and ignorant.*

When students use the word "cramming," they usually mean a fast study session during which a person studies or reads for the first time something he'll have to know for a test. In one dictionary, it is defined as hurriedly stuffing the mind full of a subject in preparation for an examination. The dictionary doesn't say whether the subject is brand new or something already covered. Either way, the "hurriedly stuffing the mind" is the major idea.

We believe the best grade results are achieved when the "hurriedly stuffing the mind" is a *review* of material you've *already covered*, rather than a rapid first exposure to brand new material. In other words, make your cramming a second reading of your text or a review of your notes and the underlined portions of your textbooks. The cramming that is a rapid first exposure might get you a C in a course, but the cramming that's a review is the kind that gets B's and A's.

Sprint on your finals

Cramming before final exams can help, and often can boost your final grade. Some people have been able to learn a whole three semester-hour course in one evening. One contributor did this. He was failing a sophomore course and made a cyclone sprint during a 12-hour non-stop cram session the night before his final exam. He aced the final and got a B in the course. This is an exceptional case, but it points out two things: students can learn a lot of material in a cram session, and final exams deserve a lot of effort.

In fact, finals can often make or break a student. D grades can turn into B's or even A's—if the instructor is especially impressed by the final sprint—and B's or A's have turned into C's and D's just because of a two or three hour final exam. Often, finals can make the difference between passing or failing a course—as in the case of one contributor. Final exams are given in order to measure your overall effort and production for the semester. So when you prepare for them, make a big sprint. A good effort before a final exam will pay off.

Getting back to cramming—allow yourself some time when you cram—even if it is only enough to cover the major points in a course.

But remember this about cramming: YOU ARE NOT GETTING THE FULL VALUE OF THE COURSE . . . especially if the cramming is a first exposure. When you cram, you don't have time to reflect leisurely upon the material or to analyze it or question it. You're aiming for one goal: *grades*.

If you can't cram, don't

There are some students who simply don't like to cram. They may just plain hate cramming, perform poorly under pressure or tend to become easily fatigued. If cramming is not for you, then don't do it. Plan your work so you don't get caught in a bind before exams and won't have to rely on "hurriedly stuffing the mind."

Some mathematics and engineering courses may be better served by a rested, alert mind than by a late show cramming session. You will have to determine this for yourself, according to your own abilities and preferences, your background knowledge and the particular course involved.

Get some sleep

If you plan to stay up most of the night cramming or doing any of your school work, make sure you actually *work*. If you're going to goof off with friends or rap half the night, forget it and go to bed. The sleep will do more for you. Even if you cram most of the night, make sure you get *some* sleep. A couple of hours sleep may make you a little loggy, but it will give you some needed rest and your thoughts will have an opportunity to sift into place. Even the most ardent "crammer" contributors agree on this: you should get *some* sleep before an exam—the more the better.

Getting some sleep reduces the chance of freezing when you enter the testing room and—for some reason—a couple of hours sleep helps reduce the interference.

The "late shows" which run all night may be necessary in a real bind, but they do reduce your work ability and can cause fatigue.

Stage fright affects many

When all is said and done—or studied and maybe learned— and you enter the classroom for a test, don't let your nervousness get the better of you. Almost everyone is a little tense before an examination. *Relax* the last few minutes before your exam. Think about something else or, if you're in another class, pay extra attention to the lecture. Students who cram until the instant the exam papers are handed out are more likely to get "shook up" than those who perhaps glance through a newspaper or have a cup of coffee.

If you clutch or freeze during an examination, speak to the instructor. Sometimes students will get "locked up" inside and draw a complete blank when they look over their exam questions. In severe clutch cases, students find they are unable to remember even the most simple points learned in a course. It is a sort of stage fright where the actor can't remember his lines. It's a case of being "uptight."

Most professional instructors are aware of this phenomenon and are sympathetic. They may permit you to leave the room for a moment and get some air. Sometimes just standing in the hallway can help. If you have a hard-nose who won't let you leave the room, then just forget the test for a few minutes. Concentrate on something else. You can even sketch a picture on a piece of scratch paper. Do *something* to get your mind off the test for a few minutes, and *don't worry about the time you're losing*. You'll waste more time and will be less efficient if you try to struggle through the test with that "locked up" feeling. Relax and be cool. Remind yourself that you're pretty smart and you have what it takes. Then, when you're calmer, pick up your exam and go to it.

Some of the factors which contribute to "clutching" are inadequate preparation, exhaustion and insufficient sleep, consuming too much coffee or sleep-inhibiting drugs, and the importance attached to doing well in a showdown.

All the preparation in the world will be virtually wasted if a student can't perform on an examination. It might be advantageous to look at some of the more common faults found in the taking of an examination.

The time is yours—use it wisely

A major mistake is making poor use of the time given for writing an examination paper. It should be obvious that an involved essay or computation problem worth, say, 20 points warrants more time than a five-point question. But, many students will ramble on with several paragraphs of material in answer to a small question and run so short of time that they have to answer a large question (in terms of points) in a few hastily scrawled sentences. Frequently students knowingly will do this because they know the answer to the short question and are vague about the larger one. They try to prove their knowledge and preparation by supporting a short question with a long answer with the hope that their inability to answer a larger question will be overlooked. This, of course, is ridiculous. A five-point question is worth only five points and that's it. Keep your sense of values when apportioning your time on an examination. Sometimes it would be smarter to write several paragraphs of "bluff" on a 20-point question than to spend your time repeating yourself and needlessly elaborating on a five-point question. That "bluff" might get you on the right track or at least net you a few points on the larger question.

An easy way to avoid spending too much time on short questions is to answer the larger questions first and save the five-pointers until the end. Instructors will usually permit students to change their answer sequences if they properly number their answers and indicate on their papers that the answers are not in numerical order.

Apportion your overall effort wisely

Putting your effort where it will count—or simply making a proper investment of your time—is even more important when it comes to planning your total study effort. Too often, students will get carried away with courses they especially like, while the unpopular or more difficult courses suffer. This is particularly true with beginning students.

Freshmen sometimes get excited about a course or two and spend all their efforts on those, leaving the more difficult and duller courses behind. Sure, it's fun to make an A in a course you enjoy, but is the effort worth it if you get poor grades in your other courses? In terms of progressing toward a degree, it would be much wiser to divert some of your extra effort into a less popular course and wind up with satisfactory grades all the way around. Chances are that if you like a course, you will do well in it anyway.

Suppose, as you are approaching final exams, you are carrying a high B in, say, psychology, but are a borderline student in algebra. Where would you best profit by spending your time? With an adequate review, you know that in all probability you'll get a good grade in psychology. Therefore, it would be much wiser to put your extra final effort into the algebra and at least pass the course.

With courses of equal weight, an A and an F will average out for a C. But you will have completed *only one course*. If the extra effort had been invested in the algebra, you might have ended up with a B and a D. These would still average a C and you would have completed *two courses*.

This may seem very elementary, but it is surprising how many students don't see it this way. It is always easier to spend more energy on an easy, interesting, or "more sensible" course than those which are rough, distasteful or have no apparent value. But sometimes it takes a little self-discipline in order to put the effort where it will best serve you.

Know how much each course is worth

Making a proper investment of your effort also involves keeping your eye on the credits. When apportioning your study time, be aware of the amount of units or credits each course is worth. Don't "blow" a five-unit course for the sake of a two- or three-unit course.

In terms of your grade average, it would pay off to spend more effort on a five-hour course than a two-hour one.

Take your time

Getting back to the topic of making proper use of your time on an examination, the author wishes to urge students to *use all the time allowed for an examination*. Taking an examination can be painful, and students sometimes have the urge to dash through the test and take off long before their time is up.

It is hard to make yourself stay there to re-read your answers or re-calculate your figures. Students want to hand in their examinations, get some air and forget the whole business. But stick around and go over your answers. In going over your work, you might discover you left out a point here or there or can improve a few sentences.

Some instructors consider it an insult to their ability to prepare exams if a student finishes early. One instructor explained, "If a student leaves early, he'd better have a good paper. It had better be well organized, legible and thorough. If his paper isn't good, I tend to grade it more stiffly than if he had used the full period, because he could have used the extra time to do a better job."

First guess is best

If your examination is the multiple choice (or multiple guess) variety, re-read the questions, but be careful about changing answers—especially those which may have been based on pure guesswork. Statistical evidence indicates that a first guess is more likely to be right than a later one.

Think before you write

When you sit down to take an essay type of examination, organize your thoughts when you formulate an answer. This will save you time because it will give you a direction in which to write. Instructors say that one of the most common mistakes made by students during examinations is their failure to think out their answers before writing. And this mistake costs points.

Some students can't seem to get thinking about an answer until they've started writing. This is frequently reflected in their answers. If you have to write something before you can get going, try writing a brief outline of your ideas and the main points of your answer.

. . . and write simply

When writing your answer—or any paper that is to be graded —you'll find it advantageous to use short, simple sentences. Sentences which ramble on and on may be hard to follow and tend to reflect *unclear thinking.* Not only do instructors sometimes get lost trying to follow a sentence that runs into paragraph length; students themselves often get lost in their own verbosity.

The use of short, simple sentences is a part of effective organization and they can be written easily if you think about an answer before you start wagging your pencil or pen.

Room for additional thought

It's a smart idea to leave some space at the end of each answer. When you re-read your paper or if you stumble across other ideas you want to include, you'll have room. By leaving sufficient room for afterthoughts, you can avoid using arrows, scratching in the margins, or the "this paragraph applies to question one" sort of thing.

In addition to complaining about poor organization of examinations, instructors say that students frequently fail to support broad generalizations in their answers. Be specific and use details or examples to support bold statements. And give a few accurate how's and why's. Students usually know enough material to support generalizations, but they're in too much of a hurry to bother with a few of the details that make the difference between a mediocre answer and an excellent one.

CHAPTER 5

Libraries, References etc.

Every student will have occasion to use a college library somewhere along the line, whether he's majoring in electrical engineering, pharmacy, English or physical education. Surprisingly enough, few students really know when and how to make use of the vast resources in a library. If you need some supplementary information in a hurry or face a deadline for a term paper or other research project, you'll be way ahead if you know how to find information quickly. Students who wait until they're pressed for time to learn how to tap the library's resources can expect to waste a lot of that time just learning their way around and trying to find a reference.

If you don't know your way around the library—or how to get your hands on some reference material quickly—it might pay you to spend a free hour or two just browsing through the library and card catalogs. And if you don't know how to use the card catalog or locate a book, ask a librarian. Some may brush you off, but many will give you a good check-out.

Conventional catalog systems list material alphabetically under three major headings: the subject, the title, and the author.

Periodical literature

Don't overlook the *Readers' Guide to Periodical Literature* when you are given a research project. Relatively new subjects and topics which are currently controversial or much discussed are often covered in depth in magazines and larger newspapers. One student who was assigned to study welfare systems and the "War on Poverty" had to draw most of her information from magazines on file at the campus library. The *Readers' Guide* was her key to finding information.

If you're seeking information about subjects which were in the news during the past 50 years or so, you might consider using the newspaper microfilm file if your library—or one nearby—has one.

Use other libraries freely

Don't hesitate to use another library if your campus library does not have adequate resources. Colleges usually have reciprocal user arrangements with nearby municipal libraries or those on other campuses. Perhaps another library will not permit you to take home references, but they'll probably let you peruse the material inside the facility.

If you're trying to locate a specific book that is not available —or has already been checked out—at your campus library, you can sometimes save yourself a lot of trouble by merely calling other libraries to see if they have a copy on file.

Grab those books early

Here's another suggestion: If you're given a research topic that has also been assigned to several other students, *get to the library early*. Many students tend to wait until the last week or even the last few days to work on a report or research project. Consequently, there may be a shortage of resource material during those few days before the deadline. There are probably millions of graduates—including this author—who have experienced the anguish of tramping to the library two or three days before a research project is due—only to discover that the best books on the subject have been checked out for the next two weeks. Unfortunately, few instructors are swayed by the excuse that good references are not available—especially if they assigned the project several weeks in advance.

Basic, low-cost references

No matter what you major in, you are bound to have occasional need of some basic reference material.

A *good dictionary is recommended for every student.* If you don't have one, get yourself a good, fat dictionary. Vest pocket "quickies," paperback dictionaries and $1.95 hardbounds may be all right for secretaries checking spelling, but they are *not suited for college work.*

In fact, many of these very low-priced abbreviated dictionaries can actually render a disservice to the user, through the use of partial synonyms—definitions which are sometimes misleading.

For example, a random glance through a low-priced vest pocket dictionary shows the word "concise" defined simply as "short."

A reader who stumbled across "concise" could probably substitute "short" and come up with a fair understanding of the sentence. But he still would not have the ability to use the word himself if he assumed that "concise" and "short" were interchangeable. One could hardly refer to a "concise" pine tree or say that a shopping center is located just a "concise" distance from campus.

Another pocket-sized dictionary defines "concise" as "brief." (We had a concise rainstorm. . . . ? He was wearing only his concises when the guests arrived. . . .?)

Abbreviated dictionaries tend to leave out multiple forms of words—plural, adverbial, etc., so their use even in checking spelling is limited (i.e., does it end in "ly" or "ally" and does the plural form end with "s" or "es"?)

And, of course, those which carry only 5,000 or 25,000 of the most frequently used words are extremely inadequate when you're dealing with scholarly words that are not common.

Good dictionaries are available at less than $10 and will serve the user for years after college. Many publishing firms offer thick dictionaries that are constantly revised to keep abreast of new words and new uses of existing words.

"Webster's New World Dictionary of the American Language, College Edition," is an excellent volume containing nearly 2,000 pages and reasonably priced. One contributor noted that this dictionary not only defines the word "eye" but also gives a detailed diagram of the human eye. True, few students will need an elaborate diagram of a human eye. The point is that a good dictionary is *thorough* in its offerings.

Good dictionaries also contain bonus information, such as lists of all U.S. colleges and universities, tables of weights and measures, charts showing the origins of languages, guides to pronunciation of English and foreign syllables, forms for preparation of formal letters, world maps and other useful reference material.

The meaning and use of words

In your college reading, try to determine the meaning of unfamiliar words through the context. This is how we learn most of our working vocabulary anyway. If you're unable to determine the meaning of a word through its use, look for it in the dictionary and become familiar with the word—its pronunciation, spelling, and definition. This is especially important if the word occurs repeatedly.

If you are trying to read something written by an author who likes to impress his readers with a million ten-letter words, don't look up all of them. Look up only those needed to help you understand the main points.

Some reading is tough

Unfortunately, some writers—particularly in the social sciences —tend to use "socialese" or "gobbledy-gook"—an awkward way of saying in 50 words what could be said more easily and clearly in 10 words. And these scholarly individuals use 10- and 15-letter words where they could have used five- or six-letter words.

A scholarly article which was required reading in an anthropology class contained a sentence which started, "With complete academic equanimity, we could reiterate the assertion that it is not altogether inconceivable that . . ."

The whole phrase (and keep this in mind when you're writing) could have been replaced with "It's possible that . . ."

This particular article was written by a young professional who apparently knew his field better than he knew the basic rules of composition.

Almost every student will run across a book or article (or maybe several) that is just impossible reading material. And sometimes a student will become thoroughly shaken by the experience.

Throw away the shell

Well, don't sweat it. Try to pick up the major messages and pass over the non-essential wordage. Regard it as a peanut, where you have to throw much of it away in order to get the meat.

While a few highly acclaimed writers are noted for their particularly flowery and complicated writing, many of the non-literary writers who murder the English language are people who really have the least to say.

Watch the simple details

If you are writing a paper and are uncertain about the spelling of a word, *look it up* in the dictionary. Spelling errors suggest an *overall carelessness* in preparation as well as *ignorance or laziness* on the part of the offending student.

One contributor lost 20 points on a *bacteriology* class term paper because he misspelled "diphtheria" by leaving out the first "h". The professor wrote on the paper: "If you don't know how to spell the subject you have no business discussing it."

Another—a political science senior—was knocked down one letter grade on a term paper because on four occasions he misspelled the name of the former Soviet Premier Khrushchev. The first misspelling was circled and labeled "disgusting!"

Still another contributor had an English instructor who announced at the outset of a junior year course that he would put a failing grade on any outside assignment containing a spelling error. (Our contributor said the professor thoroughly backed up his threat.)

The professor explained, "On tests, I'm forgiving. You're under pressure and a time limit, and you won't have access to a dictionary. So I'll let a couple (of errors) go by. But on my outside assignments, you'll have plenty of time and access to all the references you need to check yourself. A spelling error is something you can avoid. Don't make any."

Some professors are not sticklers for spelling and grammar, and look instead for content. But you'll notice that the most conscientious teachers will spot errors and point them out with a pen mark even if they don't downgrade a student's paper.

They take it seriously

Good teachers, whether they are ranked as instructors or full professors, like to consider themselves *educators*. As such, they feel responsible for appraising and correcting all facets of a student's work . . . whether it is basic content of an assignment, the structure of a student's paper or something which seems so petty as spelling.

Why the emphasis on something as "petty" as spelling? Because a college graduate, whether he is an English major, mathematician or an aeronautical engineer, is expected to be adept in *communicating*.

Get an almanac

Another valuable reference for almost all students, in addition to a good dictionary, is an annual almanac. These are available in inexpensive paperback form and contain a million handy little facts, who's who data, important statistics, dates, figures and charts. *The World Almanac* and the *Information Please Almanac* are somewhat similar and are revised annually. However, the basic information is carried forward each year, and unless the student needs very up-to-date information, one copy should suffice throughout college. It is an interesting and enlightening experience just to browse through these almanacs —not only for college work but for your general knowledge. Even if you refer to an almanac on just a few occasions during your college career, the time you save by avoiding a trek to the library should more than offset the cost.

A dictionary and an almanac are recommended as basic references for all students, regardless of their fields of study. Beyond these are additional specialized reference books relating to particular fields. You are best able to determine the additional and basic reference books you should buy.

Going a step beyond

A survey of the real grade-getters, the academicians, showed that these students not only learn what is expected, but frequently go beyond the minimum and study additional material on their own. What a chore! As if it isn't enough to try to perform the minimum—when you have several instructors who seem to think theirs is the only course you're taking.

Alas, for most of us, doing the extras is nearly impossible. We have enough trouble keeping up on a day-to-day basis.

Okay, perhaps you don't have time to read four or five extra books for additional insight into something you are studying. But certainly you leaf through newspapers and magazines occasionally. When reading periodical material, make a point of spotting articles relating to any course you're taking or expect to take. Then read these articles.

If you have access to other books relating to courses you are taking, occasionally browse through them or read a chapter or two.

Then, on a test, make reference to this outside material you've read if it is applicable. THIS CAN PAY UNEXPECTED DIVIDENDS. It serves to give you additional knowledge and insight, naturally, and it also shows you go a little beyond. It shows you're interested, alert and possess initiative.

This does not mean you must have covered all the assigned

material before you venture into the world of outside reading. Even if you are remiss in your assigned work—although you shouldn't be—outside reading can help.

Fast reviews in paperbacks

Many paperback firms put out handbooks covering particular courses. Although these books may not be prescribed for your courses, most college bookstores carry them. Such paperback booklets often jam *piles of summary information into a short space*. When you're in the bookstore, look at the paperback offerings and skim through those which may cover material you're studying. If they look like they have a lot of valuable information, buy and read them at your leisure.

Key points that are scattered through hundreds and hundreds of pages in a thick textbook are often summarily discussed in a paperback, and in a lot fewer pages.

Paperbacks are not recommended as substitutes for textbooks, but if you've fallen by the wayside and are behind, these paperbacks can be worth their weight in gold before exams.

Also, if you've gotten lost in a tough course, paperbacks can sometimes give you a *fresh approach or new insights* into understanding your subject matter.

Even if you have kept up with your regularly assigned work, paperbacks can give you new ideas, clarify old ones, and serve as extra material to draw upon when taking an examination.

Some students have found it very helpful to refer to another textbook written for the same general course. If you're stymied by the assigned textbook in a particular class, you might find a different and more easily understood approach in another textbook.

Showing interest in your major

When you've settled in a major field of study, it can be extremely beneficial to read trade or professional magazines. All fields of engineering, teaching, journalism, medicine, chemistry, pharmacy, nursing, dentistry, the "ology" sciences, art and a host of other fields have one or more nationally circulated professional journals which provide information for the practitioner and keep him up to date in his field.

Information gleaned from reading a professional journal in your field will broaden your perspective.

They provide material you can readily draw upon in an exam, during class discussion, when writing a paper, and even when you're looking for ideas for writing term papers.

And when an instructor sees that you got your material from reading a professional journal, it will make a good impression.

It will make you appear really interested in that field—and why shouldn't it? In all probability, you chose the field because you *are* interested.

Regardless of your performance academically, frequent browsing through a trade journal looks good. No, looks aren't everything, but they count. Instructors, after all, are people.

CHAPTER **6**

Term Papers, Themes, Reports

During a college career, most students will be assigned term papers or reports. Some students may have only one or two a year; others may be assigned as many as nine in one quarter or semester. At the outset of a term, it is pretty easy to forget all about them or dismiss them from the mind—especially if they're not due until the end of the term.

But, doing this may bring a final examination week during which a student stays up all night—not studying, but rapidly typing any half-way appropriate material he can find in the piles of books around him. Such last-minute efforts don't permit the luxury of a first draft or a concern for proper grammar, spelling or conformity to standard term paper style. The result is a hastily pepared mess that is handed in because *something* has to be handed in. Often, students who have cranked out a "quickie" term paper do little more than a fast rewrite job of some of the chapters in their reference books. A student who does this is taking a big risk. Not only is his grade at stake, but his reputation is on the line as well. Instructors who spot or suspect plagiarism can be pretty tough, and the newly-acquired reputation will extend way beyond the term paper. In some schools, plagiarism is regarded as cheating and is grounds for expulsion.

The best way to avoid term paper traumas is to begin work on them early—several weeks in advance. By doing this, you'll have enough time to hunt up the needed resource material, scan it for appropriate information, form a rough draft and finally to write a clear, well-organized and clean paper.

Don't pad the paper

When you're writing the paper, don't pad in unnecessary material or repeat yourself needlessly for the sake of presenting a lengthy paper. Few instructors want to wade through 30 or 40 pages from every student—especially if the paper rambles and could have been written in 10 or 20 pages. Padding just wastes their time and yours.

Don't pad your bibliography, either. A reference list citing 30 or 40 books that obviously have not all been used will usually be eyed with some degree of skepticism by instructors. After all, who has the time to read that much when preparing one routine term paper or short research report? In most instances a list of five to ten books which have been well used, as shown by your paper, will be more appreciated and more easily believed.

Neatness is the paint job

Naturally, term papers and reports should be neat—whether they're typed or written longhand. A limited amount of editing, where corrections are penned in carefully, is usually acceptable. Some instructors will flatly refuse to accept messy papers. It's true that technically your paper should be graded on content rather than appearance. But instructors are people, and may not be too impressed by the quality of the product if it's poorly wrapped. A little gloss and some salesmanship—through a neat-appearing paper—show a little extra effort and help in promoting your work.

It also pays off to follow a standard term paper form, using proper footnoting technique and bibliography organization. Remember to attribute the big, bold statements, whether you quote them directly or merely paraphrase them.

Using a little care in applying these suggestions will go a long way toward getting good grades on term papers. They're sort of like the paint on an automobile. If a car looks good, you just naturally expect it to run well; if it has a poor appearance, you don't expect much performance from it.

The topic and the length

Although some instructors suggest a length for term papers and assign or approve topics, many prefer to give students a completely free hand and decline to discuss these matters. In this event, spending a few extra minutes of your time choosing a topic and its scope can have more effect on your grade than several extra hours of research.

Whenever students asked him how long term papers should be, one English literature professor used to shrug his shoulders and ask, "How long should a man's legs be?" When his students swapped amused glances, he would say, "A man's legs should be long enough to reach the ground." His point, of course, was that a paper should be long enough to cover the subject adequately. This in itself implies that the scope of a paper should be somewhat confined. A student who picks "A Study of the Civil War" as the topic for a term paper is headed for trouble. It would be impossible to cover such a vast subject properly in a term paper. The smart thing to do would be to break down the subject. A student could do a much better job if his topic was "Economic Factors Leading to the Civil War."

In the process of teaching students to analyze, teachers look for conclusions and observations in reports and term papers. Don't merely mimic facts in writing your paper, but try to *draw a conclusion* supported by the facts stated in your paper. A conclusion can usually be worked into your summary.

Explore both sides

If you begin your paper with a hypothesis or supposition in which you present a particular interpretation or point of view, be sure to bring in contrary evidence, if there is any, somewhere in the paper. As you present information supporting or proving your hypothesis, you must also offer available contrary information and analyze it honestly. If you find that it is irrelevant, poorly thought out, the result of inadequate research, etc., you should show this.

Failure to show you have at least examined contrary information is indicative of poor or biased research.

Take a mild interest

If you're given a choice in selecting a term paper topic—or are given some latitude within a defined range of subjects, try to pick something which could interest you or at least offers you a challenge. Those who get a fair share of term papers will undoubtedly get topics which are of no interest to them. If this happens, regard it as a challenge and chalk it up as part of your over-all education—just as you would courses that don't particularly interest you. It sounds trite, but it is a matter of developing a willing attitude. If you can cultivate an interest in, or develop a positive attitude toward the assignment, you'll do a better job and you'll be less inclined to wait until near deadline—when you're forced to throw something together.

One male contributor, because of a scheduling difficulty, found himself in a course entitled "Family Structure" during his senior year. As if that wasn't enough, he was assigned a topic to top all topics for his term paper: "Find out if a mother's socioeconomic status can affect her attitude toward child rearing practices and toilet training."

Not only was he uninterested, he was downright embarrassed and angry about the whole thing.

A sympathetic friend in whom he confided the nature of his unpleasant task suggested, "That'll be a hell of a conversation-maker some day, you'll probably look back and laugh. Besides, any time someone cites Spock, you can start talking like an expert."

Using that consolation, the student approached the task with the idea that if he had to delve into a distasteful topic, he'd hit it head-on.

He got an A on the paper and a compliment from the instructor as well.

Are you an "expert"—?

Some instructors think that students do better work when they choose unfamiliar topics. There are several reasons for this view. If you're an "expert" or "authority" in a particular field, you may inadvertently presume that the reader shares your familiarity. Hence, you'll be apt to omit supporting background material. Second, you might have trouble attributing your information, especially if you write "off the top of your head." The basic information in a research or term paper should be supported by some authoritative source; unless you're a *recognized* expert, your word alone is not sufficient documentation.

Also, there is a possibility of inadvertently injecting personal bias when you write about a subject—particularly a controversial one—with which you are highly familiar. You may fail to support fully your point of view and to explore other viewpoints. You risk slanting your whole approach—not only in your writing, but in your research as well. Many nicely written term papers have been given low grades because the writers were involved too personally in their work.

Students who are not versed in the techniques of preparing a term paper should refer to a good, up-to-date English text or *The MLA Style Sheet*, available at most college bookstores. These will outline proper term paper format.

Many colleges, and often departments within a college or university, will prescribe a basic format for papers. It is advisable to follow carefully any recommended procedures.

Typing problems?

Students who have not learned how to type and are enrolled in a major where they're expected to turn out a voluminous amount of typed assignments, reports, research papers, theses and the like might well profit from a summer typing course or some spare time work with a self-taught touch system instruction booklet.

English and journalism majors, those seeking law degrees

and others in arts and sciences programs loaded with numerous paperwork projects could find the effort worthwhile—but not at the expense of regular study time.

Those who must rely on the laborious, plodding hunt-and-peck system to turn out reams and reams of material are apt to waste lots of precious time with the mechanics of typing and still end up with messy papers loaded with corrections.

With repeated use of a two- or four-finger h-and-p method, one *can* become proficient and learn to clip along at a comfortable 50 words a minute—but learning this is at the expense of many messy papers and much preparation time.

Many students rely on typists, who constantly run classified ads in campus newspapers, offering their services at anywhere from 20 to 50 cents a page.

CHAPTER 7

Avoiding a Nasty Jam

The mechanics of planning your courses for the next four years, two years or whatever it will take you to graduate is too involved a topic to be dealt with here in any detail. Suffice it to say that students should form at least a rough outline of their paths to graduation. Get an idea of what courses you will need and learn what courses require what prerequisite courses. Form some timetable for yourself and become familiar with the broad requirements for the degree you are seeking. If some of the courses you will have to take are real "bears," try to spread them out. Don't save all the rough stuff for the end.

Know what the degree requires

There's an old saying about "that two per cent" of the population which fails to "get the word." And most colleges across the country see their "two percenters" every June, when a small handful of seniors are advised they will not graduate on schedule because they failed—somewhere along the way—to take one particular required course or failed to meet some general requirement.

This can happen to almost any college student, either through his own or someone else's carelessness. Surprisingly, there seems to be little relationship between academic performance and failure to "get the word" on graduation requirements. Both the mediocre student and the grade-maker are equally prone to this oversight.

An outstanding student at one university discovered halfway through his last semester that he would be short a single required course—one that is normally taken during the freshman or sophomore year. Somehow, and he couldn't recall the circumstances, he had substituted an elective course for the required one. Although he had carried a full load through college and would have enough units to graduate, the administration refused to grant a waiver on the one required course he missed.

He was fortunate in that he discovered the oversight eight weeks before graduation. He was able to enroll in a correspondence course through his university's extension division. The work load imposed by the extra course gave him a nasty time during his last eight weeks, but he managed to complete the work and graduate on time.

While this is but one isolated case, similar instances—with less happy endings—occur every spring. Sometimes a counselor or department advisor shares the blame for the oversight, but it is *the student* who gets the short end of the stick if the administration is unsympathetic and hard-nosed. Most colleges and universities stipulate that the responsibility for meeting all requirements rests solely with the student.

Reviewing your progress

To avoid getting caught in the unfortunate "two per cent" category, periodically check your progress and make a *careful review* of your courses and your degree requirements at the beginning of your final year. If you have any uncertainties, check with your dean or department head. And if you find you've overlooked a requirement, do something about it fast.

This idea of forming a timetable and of updating it as needed can't be overstressed, because a little goof now could bring some great woes later. If you have some idea of your direction, write down a tentative program to follow through college. Don't feel rigidly bound to it, as you may change your mind on elective courses (if not the whole program) and course offerings sometimes vary from one year to the next according to demand, curriculum changes and the availability of qualified professors.

You're goofing me up

Forming a well-thought-out yet flexible course sequence can prevent not only the "two percent" difficulties just mentioned, but also the discomforting discovery many students make when they're barred from a required or preferred course because they overlooked a prerequisite.

Many junior and senior courses are open only to students who have taken certain preliminary and foundation classes. One contributor recalls coming out on the short end of the following dialogue—one typical of those occurring at sign-up desks each registration period on almost every campus:

I'M SORRY, MR. GREEN, BUT YOU CAN'T TAKE ANTHROPOLOGY 406. YOU HAVEN'T TAKEN AN-THROPOLOGY 201.

"What's Anthro 201?"

CULTURES OF MAN.

"Oh, well—I took Sociology 232. We sort of covered cultures."

I'M AFRAID THAT ISN'T ADEQUATE.

"Look, I've *got* to have an upper division anthropology course."

YOU MIGHT TRY ANTHROPOLOGY 300—EVOLU-TION—IT'S OPEN TO ALL JUNIORS AND SENIORS.

"Well, I would, but I can't. It's offered at the wrong time. That's when I have to be in History 307."

I'M SORRY, MR. GREEN. PERHAPS YOU CAN TAKE HISTORY 307 *NEXT* TERM.

"But I can't. I'm a history major. I've got to take it *now* or else I can't take History 455 next term. It's a required course in my major."

ALL RIGHT. WE CAN MAKE AN EXCEPTION. YOU CAN TAKE THE ANTHRO 406 NOW IF YOU ALSO

SIGN UP FOR THE PREREQUISITE. YOU CAN TAKE
THEM TOGETHER.

"You just don't understand. I haven't got room in my schedule for your doggone Anthro 201. It'll goof everything up.
YOU'RE goofing everything up!"

SORRY, GREEN. YOU SHOULD HAVE DONE SOME
PLANNING. PLEASE STEP ASIDE—OTHERS ARE
WAITING. NEXT STUDENT, OVER HERE PLEASE!

*   *   *   *

If you've gone through this, the windy dialogue will no
doubt strike home. Sometimes, in computerization and elec-
tronic registration processing, the dialogue doesn't come until
after the student has started the class. He gets a processed
card directing him to call the dean's office about an irregu-
larity.

(Our example is not from the imagination. Some of us have
our registration campaign ribbons. We're not proud to wear
them. Don't you get any.)

Suppose our student in the preceding example had been
able to follow the alternative suggested by the registration
clerk and had signed up for "Anthro 300—Evolution," the
open course. His problem would be solved and he'd be back
on the road? Maybe. And maybe not. He might find himself
competing with a class full of advanced Anthro majors (who
have good backgrounds to draw upon) and facing a professor who gears the lectures accordingly.

But at least there would be some fancy footwork patterns
open to him to help him make the best of a nasty situation.
We'll explore these in a section entitled "A Fish Out of
Water."

CHAPTER **8**

Choosing or Changing Your Major

If you plan to be a physician, physicist, engineer, pharmacist or some other highly specialized professional, you'll have to make some big decisions and do some careful planning early. But if you're not quite sure what you want to major in, you'll have a little time to decide. Nevertheless, time has a way of flying by, and sooner or later, a college student finds he must commit himself to a major course of study. Don't get rattled if you find yourself uncommitted or unable to decide, yet rapidly floating to a point where the stream divides. If you are uncertain which way to go—despite aptitude tests you should have taken—start thinking about areas that interest you. If you major in any of dozens of liberal arts fields, it will not mean that you are stuck there for the rest of your life.

Business, government and industry, for example, are full of people with degrees in English, foreign languages, education, journalism, philosophy, literature, history, geography, geology, biology, anthropology, psychology and so on, as well as those with degrees in business or economics. There are many people working in fields other than those in which they hold degrees.

What are the needs—and opportunities?

The present day pressure toward early specialization can be hard on a student. Many drop out of college simply because they cannot bring themselves to the sometimes awesome task of making a choice. If you're in this boat, you might find it a little rewarding to check with a college placement service to see what degrees various firms are seeking when they hire new talent. The variety might surprise you!

Most firms in the general business world will consider hiring graduates from any liberal arts field and even specialty schools. This is because many companies have their own training programs. *Your degree shows them that you have a basic education, some ambition and drive, and the ability to learn. It shows you have learned HOW TO THINK.*

If you're interested in finding a field where your training and abilities would be in demand, consult some of the various books and pamphlets—and even magazine articles—which list the projected labor demands. Many publishers, and even the federal government's printing office, offer books showing occupational outlooks and the areas where trained college graduates are most needed. Many such publications even list current salary expectations and advancement prospects in each field. Also covered in these books are the various fields you could get into after securing a particular degree. For example, suppose you do well in English courses and have a flair for writing or speaking. A solid college background in English could conceivably lead to any of the following fields—to name just a few: acting; advertising; radio and television announcing, production, directing, or writing; teaching (drama, English, literature, journalism); editing and publishing; journalism (reporting and editing for newspapers, trade journals, radio and television, news syndicates, wire services or magazines); public relations, technical writing, speech pathology, library work, law, film editing and script writing, and many positions in the general business world where an ability to communicate is vital.

Graduate schools

For those who might wish to switch fields after picking up a bachelor's degree, there are always graduate schools. These not only provide advanced instruction in a given field, but they also enable graduates to move into brand new fields. Many firms even foot the bill to send interested employees to graduate schools and specialized summer training programs.

Vocational aptitudes

If you're anxious to find a field that you might both do well in and enjoy, visit your school's counseling service. Highly trained counselors will administer a battery of tests designed to measure interest and basic ability. They'll discuss your test results with you and suggest various fields in which you *probably* would succeed. Frequently the suggestions will open up doors to fields which never occurred to you and about which you know virtually nothing.

While some students have felt they have gained little practical assistance from personality, interest and ability tests, thousands of others have been steered happily into careers which never would have occurred to them had they not visited a counseling service.

A high score in a particular vocational area does not necessarily mean you'll succeed in that major or career. Nor does a low vocational aptitude score mean you couldn't make a good go of it. There are several unknown ingredients which cannot be measured. The tests merely indicate probabilities. Give careful consideration to the findings of the interest and ability tests and to the analyses presented by counselors.

The data presented will be more valuable to you in choosing a major if you take the tests *early* in your college career. You'll have plenty of time to think about the results, to analyze yourself and even to do a little outside exploring of the various fields suggested to you. If you don't take the tests until a few weeks before you have to select a major, you'll be forced to make a snap decision without the benefit of careful consideration and exploration.

Don't be too envious

Those in college having difficulty deciding on a major often envy the determined-looking types who arrive on campus with firm ideas about where they are going.

Yet the percentage of people who form vocational objectives during their early or middle teens, follow through with the college training required, and then make lasting, enjoyable careers in that line of work is actually quite small.

Many prefer to wait until they are already in college, where they have the benefit of greater maturity, experience in academics and the guidance resources offered by the institution's staff.

Often, those forming career objectives during the impressionable and perhaps idealistic teen-age period find later that this is not at all what they want—or are able to do.

For example, a teenager might read an inspiring and glorified book about a great physician, scientist or statesman and decide right then and there he wants to follow that calling.

Or a girl reads a biography of Florence Nightingale, and with a warm glow in her heart and a tear in her eye, resolves to become a nurse. It's all very touching, but not necessarily realistic.

The student may succeed in becoming a physician, scientist or nurse—with good fortune, lasting motivation and favorable circumstances. However, he or she is working against some strong probabilities in basing a decision on such superficialities.

Look hard, think it through

Wise is the student who takes a good hard look before forming and chasing a dream—who examines the demands of a field, the work performed in it and the preparation and intellectual equipment necessary to get there.

Some students actually pick a field simply because it sounds good and has some superficial appeal, their parents like the idea, or because the accompanying title carries prestige. Seriously, there are college students enrolled in certain programs thinking, "I want to be a lawyer because—well, it sounds good."

If a student does not take the time to find out what's involved in preparing for and practicing law, engineering, medicine or whatever, he is indeed living in a dreamland—and is probably in for a sudden and maybe shattering awakening. And it would be unfortunate if he prepares for some highly specialized field and does not awaken until his junior or senior year. Even then, it does not mean the road has come to an end (as we'll see later), but it does mean some extensive readjustment is necessary.

A student who has developed a strong interest in a hobby and plans to pursue it at a higher level as a career should acquaint himself with the higher level tools of the trade.

Hobbies versus professions

One student was an electronics whiz in high school—at the skilled worker level. He worked part time for a radio repair center, helped assemble custom high fidelity sets, was an amateur radio operator and says he was able to repair almost any radio. He planned on majoring in electrical engineering.

He was a mediocre math student in high school and was neither interested nor naturally gifted in the realm of thinking with numbers and symbols. Aptitude tests reflected this inability, too. Although he was aware his program would involve extensive mathematics, he brushed aside the warning signals, believing that his knowledge of electronics would offset his ineptitude and disinterest in mathematics. He bullheadedly enrolled in an engineering school—and was out on his ear a year later, glad to be out.

Looking back, he says he simply failed to reckon with the demands of the field—to acknowledge that mathematics is the tool of the engineer.

He became a history teacher and says that the only consolation from his disastrous experience is that he'll never look back wondering if he could have been an engineer. (He still enjoys electronics—as a *hobby*.)

The student with uncertainties about choosing a career is better off in a liberal arts program where he will get a good smattering of many fields, broad overall learning, can defer a commitment and does not become so highly specialized.

See those who know

In addition to taking vocational, personality and aptitude tests, the student contemplating a particular major with some uncertainty should talk with people in that field, read appropriate trade or professional journals and other material dealing with the vocation, and talk with faculty members.

Businessmen, professionals, and other working graduates are usually more than willing to give an hour or so to a college student. If you don't know any such people, flip through the yellow pages of a telephone directory and call a few individuals (or firms) engaged in work that looks interesting to you. Ask for a chance to meet with them.

If you're toying with the idea of becoming a chemist or of declaring yourself as a chem major, an afternoon talking with chemists or touring a nearby chemical research facility with a staff chemist might give you the evidence you need in arriving at a decision.

Say you enjoyed a freshman or sophomore accounting course and think the field offers possibilities. Go talk with some CPA's, auditors, company accountants and tax specialists.

Talk with *good* students majoring in fields that look attractive to you. Ask about their courses, glance through their textbooks. And consult with faculty members in those departments—a dean, his assistant or some of the professors. Faculty members can give you an unprejudiced rundown of the courses you'll get, the demands of each and some insights into working in the field itself.

Explore any ideas offered by students, working people and

faculty members—or those you develop yourself—that would further help you get a survey of the field.

If some of the material you uncover strongly discourages you from selecting that major, pass it by. You'll be better off than those who have to change signals half way through the game.

A major change in changing majors

Suppose you *have* picked a major and are having serious difficulty pursuing that course of study or perhaps feel it is not for you. What then? Consider making a change as soon as possible, assuming you've given the field and yourself a fair try.

The sooner you can make a change, the less readjustment will be involved. Sometimes one who is capable of handling the material but who lacks interest in the field can get deeply committed, particularly in the specialty fields. Making a change in those instances can cost a lot of time and money. Even then, the change may well be worth the trouble in terms of finding satisfaction in one's occupation.

Usually, a mismatch doesn't take long to discover. The warning signs generally show up early. The most common ones are a complete lack of interest in the field and an ineptitude in the key courses.

If, for example, you are majoring in physics but feel you are just not meant to be a physicist, look around for another field of study before your grades start reflecting your inability or lack of interest. A poor grade average will stay with you, even if you switch fields, so get out before you do too much damage.

Sometimes a family member—or a student himself—will have his heart set on his becoming an engineer, physician, physicist, accountant or other professional. In this case, changing majors might cause problems. But if one hasn't the ability or interest in a particular field, it will show up eventually, and the disappointment will probably be much greater.

Students can be pretty badly shaken to discover that they don't have the necessary mental equipment to succeed in the areas of their strongest interest. Often, through pure sweat and perseverance, a student is able to develop his talents to meet the demands of a particular major. But many students are not able to overcome their inability to handle some specific field. If you're in this situation, don't let it ruin your life or your plans to get a college degree.

Switching does not mean quitting

A surprising number of highly successful people in all fields of endeavor have miserable failures in their records. The biographies of many prominent people frequently show cases of total failure in some of their early aspirations.

Don't regard changing majors as a case of "quitting." Rather, look at it as a positive move intended to make your interests and abilities serve you better.

Naturally, before you actually switch majors, you should discuss the situation with a department head or some of your instructors. Based upon their training, their knowledge of you and the experience they've had with hundreds of students, they will be able to give you a frank evaluation of your abilities, in relation to the demands that will be placed on you in the major.

How's your background?

Inability should not be confused with ignorance—or, more politely stated—with a poor background. If you're in a scientific field, for example, and your problem is an inadequate math background, you could take a remedial math course. Often, high school students neglect certain courses they should take in order to prepare adequately for college. And, unfortunately, many high schools have deficient college preparatory programs.

Taking an elementary or remedial course in order to beef up your background might cost you a summer or an extra semester in college. So might thinning out your class load. The occasional advantages of taking more than four years to get a degree will be discussed in a later chapter.

Sometimes changing majors will set a student back a semester or two—particularly those who switch during their sophomore or junior years. If it has to be done, do it; don't worry about the time set-back. Keep your eye on a degree and not on the inconveniences you encounter along the way. Remember that life is a long race.

CHAPTER 9

Counselors, Drop-Outs, and Tough Courses

The psychologists may want to grind a white rat into our hamburger for this one, but it has to be said.

Don't rely *too much* on initial college placement tests when you select specific courses, or on aptitude tests when you select a major *IF* your past experience seems to discredit the test results.

It's one thing to figure out how long it took six workers to build three ships when it rained four days and one man worked twice as fast as the others. It's an entirely different matter getting through a tough course in calculus or differential equations. If you test well in a particular field and have been able to make *good grades* in that area, fine. But if a battery of tests show you have a keen mathematical ability, yet you traditionally pulled low grades in high school or college math (or whatever courses correspond to the test) think twice about selecting specific courses and your major.

Accept advice with care

Often, upon entering college, students who do well on math or English placement tests will be encouraged to enroll in honors or advanced courses. If you did well in high school

English or math, it might be fine to take the advanced classes. If you did poorly, be careful in selecting those classes.

Those tests in English, math or whatever fail to show a wealth of information, such as your *motivation*, your rate of learning in that area, your interest and a dozen other factors which figure into your grades or success in a particular area of study.

Frequently, the counselors offer this advice to the student who scores high on the aptitude test but does poorly in the classroom: "You are capable of more advanced work than you've been getting in class. You have not been challenged. Therefore you are bored with the subject matter and find it difficult to apply yourself."

Then follows the advice to enroll in an advanced or honors course where one's ability will be challenged.

If this happens to you and you agree with the advice, fine. Take the advanced course. You'll learn more and may do much better. But if you disagree with the advice, brother, watch out! Use your own judgment and don't rely *wholly* on the suggestions of a counselor. His job is giving you advice and perhaps new insights. He is not expected to plan your future and he does not have to share the consequences with you. Your grades go on *your* record, not his.

Ineptitude or laziness?

It is not the author's intent to discredit counselors. Their suggestions are often very valuable and can sometimes spell the difference between success or failure. Frequently, counselors can spot as *pure laziness* what you may think is an ineptitude. Give their advice careful consideration, but make sure YOU make the decisions.

The drop-out

Students wandering aimlessly through college making mediocre or poor grades frequently consider dropping out and coming back in later years. This is especially so for the student who can't settle on a major and has no real goal in college. Often, if the student is headed toward flunking out, he would be wiser to drop out voluntarily—particularly if he hopes to return to college at a later date. The reason is obvious.

Statistics indicate that the majority of college drop-outs never return to the campus. Marriage, a job and other new situations get in the way and the ex-student simply never makes it back to the classroom. Some, however, gain maturity, a set of goals and new drive while away from the campus and come back with a new gusto.

Are you qualified?

One easy way to avoid academic difficulties and poor grades is to determine in advance whether you're qualified to take a particular course about which you have some reservations. If you're not sure your background is adequate or if you doubt your ability to handle a course, talk with someone in the department—preferably the instructor who teaches that particular course. Tell him your background and grades in courses related to the one in question. College faculty members are usually helpful in offering their appraisal of your potential in a course. If they think you'd be in for a tough time, they'll let you know, and perhaps they'll offer some good suggestions.

Bail out—now!

Sometimes a person will enroll in a class which—right off the bat—leaves him behind in a spinning state of confusion. If you jump into something that is way over your head, discuss it with the instructor *immediately*. The instructor may suggest background reading or he might even advise you to drop the course. If you drop a course during the first week, you'll usually have time to enroll in something else. Most colleges will permit students to drop courses with no consequences if they do it *before* the first scheduled exam in that class. If you don't drop the course until after the first exam —and if you fail the exam—it may be permanently recorded on your transcript. . . . a big "F."

Our old theme

Again, we're back to the old theme of "asking"—of making the personal contact with an instructor. Sometimes it is difficult to make this contact—especially for the new student in a huge class at a large institution. In the smaller schools, it is easier to make the personal contact and to seek advice. But in the large schools where students are assigned six-digit registration numbers and attend classes of 100 to 200 students, it takes real push to break away from being just another number. Well, *make that push* if you haven't already. Be *you*, don't be just another figure on a data processing card. If other students are content to be "matriculation number 157186," let them take the consequences. Stand out a little.

A fish out of water

Frequently, juniors and seniors—through no direct fault of their own—wind up in classes where they are completely out of their element.

As a student progresses in college, he's apt to have less flexibility in selecting "elective" classes to fulfill broad degree requirements, as we saw earlier. Juniors and seniors, for example, may have to take more advanced "electives" in order to get the upper division (junior and senior level) credit they need to graduate. And because their majors require them to attend a certain sequence of classes at specific times, they have to schedule their "electives" around their core courses.

For example, suppose a senior majoring in English has to satisfy a biological science requirement. Theoretically, he could meet the requirement by taking any of a dozen biology courses. But perhaps, in order to meet his upper division requirements, he is forced to take a more advanced biology course—one which doesn't require foundation courses and is "open" to any junior or senior. Or suppose, because of scheduling problems, the only time he has available for a biology course is 10 A.M. on Monday, Wednesday and Friday.

It's probable there won't be too many upper division biological science courses offered at that time. Consequently, he might wind up in a genetics class, as did one contributor majoring in English.

So there sits our English major in a genetics class. Even if there are no prerequisites to the genetics course, most of his classmates could be juniors or seniors majoring in biology. Perhaps there will even be a handful of graduate biology students in the class.

Realizing he's apt to have difficulty competing with advanced biology students who have a solid background, our English major would be smart if he discussed the situation with his instructor. No, he shouldn't ask for favors, but neither should he hide the fact that he's completely out of his element because of unusual circumstances. Most instructors know that such situations are very common, and most will be sympathetic and will give the student a little leeway.

Get the trouble on record

Several contributors have experienced instances of getting out of their element. They agree that it *pays off* to alert the instructor.

And obviously, in our example above, the genetics instructor is not going to be aware of the problem unless the student consults with him.

Let's be more blunt about the above situation. If your instructor knows you're a junior or senior, that you're out of your element because of complicated circumstances, and that you're earnestly trying to get through the course, he'll probably give you a satisfactory grade even if—speaking strictly objectively—you don't deserve that grade. Only a "mean cookie" would flunk a student in this situation.

Avoid the stain of a red F

Speaking of flunking—and many students get an F or two during college—do everything you can to avoid an F. Cut

down on your social life or drop out of your extracurricular
activities if you must. In order to balance one credit hour
of F, you'll have to get one hour of A or two hours of B to
average out for a C. And still, you have to make up the requirement with the same or another extra course. Besides, failing
grades are *permanently recorded* on a student's transcript.
Failing grades take a heavy toll both in terms of time and
money.

. . . and the headaches of D's

And avoid D grades in your major. Most colleges refuse to
grant credit for grades of D in one's major, and the student
has to repeat the course.

Something else about grades of D: While they are better
than failing grades, they generally are non-transferable, regardless of your overall average. Most accredited institutions
grant credit only for courses in which the transferring applicant
made a grade of C or better.

CHAPTER **10**

Taking Longer;
Going Elsewhere

Some sports authorities say a swimmer should easily be able
to go a mile in an hour or so. But a person towing a heavy
load, a poor swimmer or a dog-paddler might become exhausted
and drown if he tried to achieve that rate. And a superior
swimmer wouldn't find that rate much of a challenge.

Traditionally, the course leading to a bachelor's degree takes
four years. This has become an established idea and apparently
is based on some old-fashioned assumption that students have
nearly equal abilities and devote their full time to college
work. A few colleges are beginning to shift to a three-year
program—particularly for brighter students.

Some students with family and job responsibilities are
unable to devote their full time and attention to going to
school. What happens to them? And what about the full
time student who is just not quite able to keep up by taking
the so-called "average" class load?

Select the best pace
The answer lies in taking a little longer getting through. If
you simply cannot handle the college program in four years,

then slack off on the load. Take a little less than the "average" load.

Colleges and universities prefer four-year students. But if it takes you longer, so what? The degree still looks the same! There is nothing stamped on a degree saying "this student took an extra year to graduate." Even if you are a full time student, don't feel there is a stigma attached to spending more than four years getting that degree. The important thing is to make sure you will get the degree. A few years hence, no one will care how long it took you. The significant question will be: Did you graduate?

Schools seldom mind

Few institutions actually require the student to complete his work in four years. If you honestly believe spending a fifth year or going to summer school would make the difference, then do it. Every year, thousands of students are getting their degrees after completing a fifth year.

Often, students whose class loads overtax their abilities end up flunking a bunch of courses or pulling very low grades. As a result—if they are still in college—they have to spend longer anyway by making up courses, and the poor grades have left a big dent in the cumulative average.

Summer schools ease the load

The same goes for summer school as for the fifth year in college. Don't feel there is a stigma attached to summer school. Students who have a hard time in college frequently find it very advantageous to attend one or more summer sessions. Summer school not only can reduce the burden during the regular school year, but also can provide an opportunity for you to devote more attention to a particularly rough course.

You won't be alone in summer school. Summer programs at colleges and universities across the country are becoming increasingly popular. One reason for this is that somehow—maybe because of the weather—summer sessions tend to be more informal than regular sessions. Students flock to summer schools to accelerate their programs, to broaden their learning, to make up work, to ease the burden during the regular year, and even to participate in social activities.

Many students who are required to take a foreign language take it during summer sessions. Languages (and many other courses) can require a great deal of time and effort. Taken during the regular year, they often bog a student down and other courses suffer. One well-utilized summer in school can generally lighten the class load for two regular years. If your college or university does not offer summer courses, it would pay to check with your dean's office or department head to see what other schools offer courses for which your school will grant credit. Before enrolling in another school for summer courses, be sure the credits are transferable. And if you plan to go to another school for a summer session, take this advice: apply for admission early. It is much easier to cancel out at the last minute, should you change your plans, than to get accepted at the last minute.

Changing schools

If you want to fly to Timbuktu but can't afford a ticket in the first class section, what do you do? Take the tourist class accommodation, of course. The same goes for colleges, and while the tourist section is not so plush, it will still get you there.

Getting a degree from a top-notch institution or prestige university can be a rewarding experience. For those who like to boast, it may provide laurels for discussion throughout a lifetime. But competition is especially rugged in the prestige colleges, and many students find themselves unable to make the grade. Those headed for trouble usually become aware of it well in advance. However, there are frequently pressures —social, family, or an inner need—which compel these students to continue until they are cordially invited to the nearest exit.

A *degree is a degree*

Upon seeking a first job, a degree from a prestige institution may make a difference. But over the years following graduation, the name at the top of the diploma carries less significance.

There are thousands of good, accredited colleges across the country which offer fine educations—and degrees—even though they don't necessarily carry great names.

If a student knows he cannot make it through a prestige college, a transfer to a smaller or less competitive college would be a wise move. It may be a bitter disappointment to have to pack up the bags and go to another school, and it may even cause some momentary embarrassment. But it does not mean the world is coming to an end. And, it doesn't necessarily reflect on the student. The point is: transfer before it is too late, and get a degree elsewhere.

This advice should not be taken as a suggestion to bail out under pressure. It is intended only for those who are sincerely trying, yet know they are on a downhill path. Sure, the tougher schools require more work and a higher scale of performance. That is why they have prestige reputations.

Many students who are overwhelmed in large universities adapt more readily to smaller colleges where they are able to find a more personal relationship with the faculty and can get more individual attention.

Remember that it is easier to transfer while you are still enrolled and in good standing in an institution than it is to be admitted to another college after flunking out of the first, being placed on probation or rolling up a pile of non-transferable D's.

Give yourself the benefit of talking with a school advisor before making a decision to transfer. With some counseling, you might be able to salvage things and remain where you are. Or perhaps advisors would concur with your thinking and could even suggest other schools where you'd more likely make it to a degree.

Keep a sense of values

It is sickening to read frequent newspaper stories about college students who commit suicide or snap and run amok because of academic pressures, scholastic inadequacies or failure in something.

It seems like an absurd, senseless waste when students who fail in a particular institution or at some academic endeavor find life so humiliating or overpowering that they leap from buildings or put bullets through their heads. Academic achievement is just not that important. Sadly, so many of these unfortunates have become instilled with a false or unrealistic sense of values and have fallen victims of exaggerated pressures.

Some even calmly adopt the philosophy: If I can't become a doctor—or physicist or lawyer or whatever—and I fail, life is not worth living.

It's grim. And the statisticians say the suicide rate among collegiates is rising.

If things get that tough, we say *relax*. Change schools, change majors, change goals. Some of us had to do it. The disappointment fades in time.

Undergraduate students who need a "second chance" often enroll in the many junior colleges throughout the nation, boost their grade averages and then transfer back to larger, four-year institutions.

Several directories of U.S. colleges and universities are available giving information about institutions, programs offered, admission requirements and costs.

What's in a name . . . ?

Frequently, a student in academic trouble seeking to transfer out of a large or tough prestige college will meet strong resistance. Friends who look down their noses at what they call "podunk" colleges may say, "Aw, you don't want to go to some hokey no-name college. Why, a degree from there won't mean a thing."

Arrogant nonsense. In fact, if you were to look at biographies of perhaps 100 highly successful, well-known and respected contemporary Americans, you'd probably be surprised at the assortment of colleges they attended. Countless very prominent persons are graduates of colleges that few people living more than 50 miles away have ever heard of.

Family pressures can be terrible in this regard, especially if the family is footing the bill. One contributor graduated from a top-notch university where his father had been educated. He said he was warned in advance that if he didn't go to school there he wouldn't get a cent of help from home. But so long as he maintained a good standing at "Dad's" university, he had carte blanche as far as expenses were concerned.

Some parents seek prestige through the accomplishments of their children. They'll insist their children attend big-name schools (or enter certain vocational fields)—not for the sake of their children but for the pride of being able to boast, "My sons go to Elec. Tech." or whatever the institution happens to be. If their sons don't go there, father doesn't give them any help.

Still other parents may simply say, "Look, I'm giving you one chance. If you blow it, you're on your own."

Sometimes a student can educate adamant parents. A letter from a sympathetic faculty member who stresses the student's sincere efforts and the likelihood of better results elsewhere can temper a parent's opposition.

It's your life

One who is still unable to overcome the resistance problem and knows he's headed for an exit had better mature instantly and decide just whose future is at stake—his own or someone else's. If you *know* what's best for you, do it. After all, you're the one who succeeds or fails—and has to live with it.

CHAPTER 11

Drugs and Grades

A wide variety of drugs is available on many campuses today. The range is broad and includes ups, downs, grass, smack, psychedelics, and others too numerous to mention. They are, quite simply, a fact of life on many campuses and must be dealt with as such.

We are not qualified to advise others regarding the taking of drugs—that we leave to medical men. Nor do we view such advice as within the scope of this book. We only wish to present, in this chapter, some comments offered with regard to drugs and grades.

Ups and studying

It is not uncommon for students to take stimulants in order to stay awake for an all night cramming session or to knock out a last minute paper. The stimulants taken range from coffee, tea and cola beverages to over-the-counter caffeine-base "stay alert" tablets to stronger drugs such as amphetamines.

Earlier we stated that it is better to be tired and informed than wide awake and ignorant. This does not however mean that we encourage the taking of stimulants.

Side-effects

In addition to keeping you awake all the stimulants mentioned above (including coffee and others) are capable of producing side-effects in some people. The most common side-effects are a nervous, jittery condition and an upset stomach.

If you don't get these reactions to coffee, tea or caffeine tablets it's probably OK to use them to stay awake. However, use stimulants sparingly and for short periods. Don't take them for two days to write a paper. A few hours rest will probably improve the overall quality of the work you do. Also by limiting your intake you avoid the groggy, hung-over after effects of stimulants.

If you do get a nervous reaction or upset stomach from say coffee or the caffeine-base tablets, try candy. People who work long shifts (van drivers, pilots, ship crewmembers, etc.) say that candy with a high sugar content (mints, etc.) helps them stay awake. Frequently chewing a fresh piece of gum also helps. A short walk in fresh air can help one remove the so-called cobwebs and the desire to doze. Other suggestions offered for perking one up during the wee hours include drinking ice water, taking a cool shower and taking occasional breaks for mild exercise. One can get very hungry during an all-night work session. Some find that a midnight breakfast helps them stay awake, while others have the opposite reaction and become logy after a meal.

Amphetamines

Amphetamines were at one time commonly prescribed by doctors in this country. Medical thinking has been reversed and a much more cautious approach is now in evidence. Most doctors refuse to prescribe them for people who want them merely to stay awake. Physicians in other countries have taken a more conservative approach, and in a few countries (such as Sweden) amphetamines have been banned altogether. The side-effects of amphetamines are more pronounced than for other stimulants and your metabolism may become dependent on them.

If you're taking amphetamines to stay awake to study that's your business—it's your body and your health. We, however, strongly recommend that you try other methods of staying awake, such as those discussed above. Sometimes, when the body is crying for sleep, a nap for an hour or two will provide a great pick-up.

In any case we recommend avoiding stimulants and limiting their intake if it is necessary to take them. If they make you jittery and upset your stomach this will impair the work you do, in which case sleep will serve you better. We also suggest you consult a physician at student health for a more professional viewpoint and one which applies to your metabolism.

Turning On

As noted earlier we are neither qualified nor do we wish to deal with the subject of taking drugs to turn on. We wish only to make a few observations which some might find helpful.

You are taking a risk by using illegal drugs to turn on. Aside from risks to your physical and mental health you are risking being busted by college and/or civil authorities. A bust may mean expulsion from college and being barred from admission to another college. (All of which may drastically alter your career possibilities). This may or may not be unfair but it is a fact of life at this time and must be faced.

Very likely you may have a distorted view of the risks you are taking. The fact that a number of students on your campus take drugs and do so somewhat casually and openly may lead you to believe that the administration at your school is not overly concerned with drugs on campus. The somewhat obvious point that you may be overlooking is that even though the administration may not actively seek out and bust drug users, when a case is uncovered it will be dealt with seriously. Again this isn't very fair, but it's often the case. Furthermore, you are also under the jurisdiction of civil authorities who may take a much different view than your college.

It should be obvious at this point that we very strongly discourage "turning on." Our concern is in helping you through college and showing you ways to get better grades with less effort. And it is on that basis alone that we state our position.

Each individual must decide on his own position regarding drugs, demonstrations and other campus situations. We can only suggest that you weigh the possible consequences of your activities against your overall college goals and be aware of any risks you might be taking . . . both academic and legal.

CHAPTER 12

Winners and Losers

Birds of a feather . . . ?

Students with comparable academic performance somehow seem to gravitate together socially. Perhaps a C student could retort: "Three of my best buddies make A's"; or an A student could say: "I'm no snob. Some of my closest friends make C's."

If you vigorously disagree with our beliefs and the shoe doesn't fit, then pass it by. Otherwise, give it some consideration.

At one extreme in our observation are scholarly individuals possibly drawn together by their enjoyment of learning and their interest in academics and intellectual exchanges—as well as mutual social interests, if any. At the other extreme are poor students who subordinate the "college" part of college in a common and maybe full-time pursuit of outside enjoyment and activities.

The good or superior students who "hang around" together will undoubtedly profit academically from scholarly discussions, exchanges of viewpoints, mutual cultural pursuits, the swapping of study tips and habits, the primary emphasis given by each member to study discipline and good grades—and an overall involvement in the academic community.

A group of the more serious and better students also will adjust its socializing activities to sensible study schedules. The members will study when they have to and swing when time permits.

A group of poorer students, on the other hand, will no doubt always have some diversion going on—some form of partying or sloughing off that encourages participation at the expense of the studies.

Guilt by association

Individuals who tie in with a particular crowd *tend to be judged on the basis of the whole group*—they become typed by the reputation earned by the circle they run with. If you run with dolts, you'll be regarded as a dolt; if you go with an academically "in" crowd, you'll share the respect they've earned from other students and members of the faculty. This is especially so in smaller schools.

At a huge institution, your social ties may go unnoticed by the faculty unless these ties include other students in your major. If they do, your instructors may draw some conclusions. For example, if you're a civil engineering major and you traditionally sit in a cluster with the engineering dummies, you're taking the risk of becoming branded a dummy yourself. Sure, if you make straight A's in your work, you'll probably get an A regardless. But if you need a little break, some benefit of doubt where your class grade hovers between a B and an A, or need some advice and coaching from an instructor, your membership in goof-off corner could spoil the show. Maybe you'll say it's unfair for a professor to look at your associates when he makes judgments. So okay, it's unfair.

Educators agree

Just to check our ideas—to see if our observations were valid —we consulted with some college faculty members. They agreed and were even more emphatic about it than we are. One advisor said flatly, "The losers run with losers. Almost every time I ask a probation student how his friends are doing, he tells me they're having trouble too."

This is typical of a common pattern found in our society: *People tend to seek out their own levels.* Professional people usually prefer to socialize with other professionals—and so on.

We're not saying that you must not associate with students whose performance is equal to or less than yours; nor are we suggesting that a student sever existing social ties with such people. Your friends are your business.

Instead, we are encouraging students of poor, fair or middling performance to *form additional associations that bring them in contact with good students.*

Naturally, if a student doesn't particularly value loose ties to a group of average or poor students and can choose between that group or a bunch of better students, he might find it beneficial to drop the former group altogether. And when he's picking friends, he'd be better off choosing good students.

Talk over the classroom stuff

Beyond the "branded by association" factor is the direct help you can get from good students in your classes or major merely by talking about your subjects. It is *ideal* if you can tie up to a group containing advanced students in your major—people a year or two ahead of you. They can give you real aid—rundowns on professors, old examination questions, insights into courses you'll take, the benefit of their own experiences, mistakes, etc., and actual coaching.

We all like to teach

A *very important* factor in this idea of mixing with good students is that *people enjoy teaching.* Almost everyone who is good or experienced at something delights in teaching it to others—whether it's driving a car, playing golf, understanding mathematics or merely making good grades. In a way, helping or coaching another student is a sort of showing off (to the learner or to one's self) or of assuming a leadership role, of testing one's own ability to instill his skills in others and of examining and reviewing his own knowledge and proficiency. A person can reinforce or test his own learning by teaching.

People who are able to help usually are flattered by being asked and sense a little glow of pride in assisting—especially when the learner suddenly gets that "now I understand" look. Teaching makes a person feel important . . . trite as it may sound.

Ask, ask, ask

Just as we encourage students to ask their instructors questions, we encourage them to ask questions of other students. If you encounter difficulty in a course, *don't be embarrassed to ask your classmates a few questions.* You may find some who understand the material and can explain it to you in simpler terms.

Sometimes students are afraid to consult with classmates, just as they're reluctant to raise their hands and ask questions during lectures. They're shy and perhaps think they'll appear stupid. Ridiculous. Seeking help from good students in a class can have its social as well as academic values.

Swing or sweat?

To illustrate the picking up of good habits from a group of better students, say it's a Wednesday night and you want to go drink beer, see a movie or whatever. If your friends are not especially good or serious students, you'll probably be able to round up a handful of people, as there will always be those willing to do anything but study. But if they're good, serious students, your suggestion may get turned down by most of those you invite . . . with a blunt, "Look man, I've got tests coming up. I've got to study." So—you either go by yourself (which is not particularly enjoyable) or you think, "Phooey. I might as well study too."

What a favor they've done you by saying "No."

If you're not one to enjoy studying—or in fact find it loathsome—you'll discover that the more accustomed you become to concentrated study the less distasteful it gets, the easier it gets and the more proficient *you* become. Those who dislike studying and run around with "non-student" students will not get the chance to find this out for themselves.

CHAPTER **13**

A Happy "Home"

"Get your dirty socks out of my half of the room!"

The room and roommate situation of most students may have little bearing on academic performance *provided the relationship is a good one.* But a bad situation can cause problems.

Depending upon the sensitivity of a college student, a strained roommate relationship can taint a student's attitudes and moods. And the overall attitude toward college life, as well as one's day-to-day moods, will indirectly affect academic performance. Few people can exert their best when their home life is rocked with turmoil or full of tension. In a sense, your residence *is* your home life during college.

Living in a room where you can't study properly or are unable to get a decent night's sleep because of noise, lights and other disturbing factors can also adversely affect your grades.

Now, some students will make good grades despite the inconveniences of a strained roommate relationship or a room where conditions are not conducive to proper study. But the academic performance of *most* college students will to some degree relate to the conditions of their "home." Achieving a tolerable "home" situation, if not complete harmony with one or more roommates, is most important to a student's chances of attaining high grades.

While the more advanced students—sophomores on up—usually can choose their residences and roommates, incoming freshmen are often arbitrarily assigned rooms and roommates in dormitories. By virtue of their youth, the often random nature of roommate assignments, inexperience in sharing a room and the newness of college life, freshmen are more prone to roommate difficulties.

Uncomfortable situations, however, can arise at any stage of college life when two or more students share close quarters. You've probably heard the old saying, "anytime more than one person gets together, there will be arguments."

In a typically poor roommate situation, little phrases such as "get your dirty socks out of my half of the room" fly back and forth. The scenes which can result when roommates get at odds are often pathetically hilarious. Full-fledged arguments and even fights can erupt over such trifles as whether a window should be opened, a light left on or whether books can be left on chairs. To an observer, the little battles between roommates can be very amusing. To the participants, they constitute a very serious business.

Mature students can create a comfortable atmosphere by establishing a loose set of ground rules from the start. Sometimes a preliminary discussion is necessary. Often, very little discussion is needed if each roommate is sensitive to the other's preferences and dislikes.

Sharing a room with one or more persons is a two-way deal. Each roommate must respect the others and, in turn, can expect—even demand—similar treatment.

Early birds and night owls

People have varying habits and some have unusual living patterns. A light sleeper who goes to bed early, for example, will undoubtedly find it annoying to have a goof-off roommate who stays up late, keeps the lights on, rattles around the room or entertains friends at all hours.

Or consider this fairly common occurrence: One student

studies best late at night, perhaps staying up until the wee hours, and then sleeps in until the last minute. Put him in a room with a student who likes to sack out early in the evening and then bolts out of bed at 4 A.M. to crack the books. Unless both are very sound sleepers or gingerly tip-toe around and study outside the room, there will be problems. Each will probably regard the other as some kind of nut.

At 10 P.M., one will snarl, "For crying out loud, it's the middle of the night. Turn out the . . . lights." Six hours later the other, rudely awakened, will grumble, "Good grief, it's four o'clock in the morning. Stop making so . . . much noise."

A student who keeps up with his work and demands a good night's sleep before a final exam will probably raise havoc with a roommate who stays up all night with the lights on while cramming.

Some students like to study with a radio playing nearby while others find noise of any sort distracting. A multitude of problems can arise from such differences. Usually, students can work them out by using a courteous, mature approach, a little tact, and if anger arises, a cooling off period.

The analysis of an intolerable roommate situation need not concern us here. If a problem exists, a student should try to get it straightened out before it gets out of hand, either in his mind or in reality. Start by talking it over with your roommate or roommates. Often, a roommate is not really aware he is contributing to a problem.

In discussing roommates, we are not especially concerned with the question of whether you *like* your roommate. A close friendship between roommates is not necessarily requisite to a tolerable situation. What's important is that you are *able to study and sleep without interference*.

Living at a circus?

Regardless of where you live, whether it's a dormitory, boarding house, fraternity or sorority house, student apartment, etc.,

make sure the activities of your roommates and neighbors
don't cut into your study effectiveness or sleep. It's hard for
any student to study in or near a din of jabber, hi-fi sets, electric guitars and some of the other noises associated with group
living. If the noise is impossible, change rooms or find somewhere else to study.

Some students will undoubtedly get an unusual person or
oddball for a roommate—someone with objectionable or ob-
noxious habits. This is bound to happen when large numbers
of students are herded together into student living quarters.

So—if there is a real problem, what should you do?

First, find a place where you can study effectively. Most
campuses have student study lounges where noise is kept to a
minimum. Libraries are usually good, as the atmosphere is
academic and quiet.

Meanwhile, try to iron out the problem with your roommate, bearing in mind that he, too, has his rights. If you're
unable to resolve the problem, speak to a counselor if you
live in a dormitory or someone with authority if you live elsewhere.

Don't be a fink

Frequently, problems can be resolved when someone with
authority arbitrates. Perhaps your arbitrating authority or you
yourself can suggest that you change rooms. Here, we are discussing the situation with the assumption that your roommate
is at fault and that you are the innocent victim. It is always
easy to blame someone else for a difficult situation. If you
have serious problems with more than one roommate, you
should consider requesting a single accommodation. Some
students simply do not get along well with others in close
quarters. True, single accommodations may cost a little more
than doubles or multiples, but that is the price of solitude.

The two extremes

Two contributors said their worst semesters, in terms of

grades, arose from poor rooming situations. One was a western girl who grew up on a farm. At the beginning of her sophomore year at an eastern women's college, she was assigned to a room with two apparently snobbish, sophisticated city girls who had gone to high school together. The two had expected a double—only to learn after paying their fees that the room was a triple.

The western girl was resented as an "intruder" from the moment she arrived, suitcases in hand. Her different background, slight accent and country manner made it worse. She was there on a scholarship, had a strong career motivation, took college seriously and was pretty. Her roommates, however, were "party girls" not particularly interested in academics, and not very pretty.

Our contributor said the semester was thoroughly miserable. She was the constant victim of a two-to-one conspiracy, malicious pranks and a few instances of downright meanness— where her mail was intercepted and read aloud to a gaggle of giggling girls.

Instead of belting her "roomies" in their faces or, more properly, seeking a room change, she tried to ride out the ordeal and her grades plunged. It was impossible for her to study in her room, and she said the whole unpleasant experience made her a nervous wreck. She received a change in room assignment at the end of the semester, but by then her grades had suffered already. Her advice is simply: "If it's a bad show, move out."

Most students are spared the discomfort of a severely strained roommate situation. Some hit the other extreme, as did the victim of another "bad" situation—where roommates are average students and good friends who tend to rap or otherwise waste time at the expense of their grades.

We have a contributor who cites this experience:

A friend and I rented a small furnished cottage. It was a

little run down, so we agreed to paint it in exchange for a month's free rent. We built and stocked a bar and painted the place when we should have been studying. We bought a second-hand television set and turned the place into quite a pad, inviting our friends to stop in for a snort anytime.

It was the great life. We were both 19 and living totally free of authority for the first time. The whole thing was very sophisticated . . . and disastrous.

At first, we laid down careful "rules" for ourselves. But these lasted about one evening. We watched television, played poker, drank beer and vowed on week nights to catch up on our school work on weekends. But every weekend, we'd agree to really get down to business the next week, again putting everything off.

We were both in terrible shape after six weeks, just before the first slate of exams. My roommate, a physics major, was so far behind he withdrew from school to avoid ruining his record.

I stayed with it, but never really got back on my feet. I spent the next 10 weeks trying to catch up, only to wind up with an F, two D's and two C's. That put me on probation.

Acting on the advice of a counselor, I moved into a student rooming house the next term and purposefully chose from among my acquaintances a congenial roommate with an excellent school record. Being around a roommate who insisted on studying a lot, who frequently talked about his school work and who gave me a number of helpful ideas made a world of difference and my grades started going up. His academic qualities seemed to rub off and they stuck. It wasn't until my senior year that I tried independent living again. By then I was mature enough to discipline myself, had developed good habits, and had no trouble.

His experience—with the second roommate—again demonstrates the value of associating with good students.

Choose wisely

If you're choosing roommates from among friends, select ones who are serious about college and who make good grades. If you're a good student yourself, you'll be better off sharing your quarters with someone who is as concerned as you with maintaining a good average. And if you're one who is inclined to goof off, all the more reason for rooming with a friend who *can* resist the temptation to stow the books and seek diversions.

There are many students who—left to themselves with no distractions—would utilize their time studying. But given the distractions of a roommate or friends who are not inclined to study and *poof* . . . down the tubes.

Freedom, fun and flunking

Younger students are more apt to get into difficulties prompted by the independence of off-campus living where there are no rules except their own and an atmosphere that is not academic.

For many students, as the preceding experience would indicate, an unregulated off-campus domicile is a first taste of almost complete independence. The lid is off. There are no rules of "quiet hours," there may not be any student neighbors to complain about noise or evening disturbances and there are few controls over the student's behavior and activity, save his own.

The mature and sincere student will have no trouble. In fact, his studies will probably profit from the relative isolation or solitude of an unregulated off-campus house or apartment. But an immature student is inviting trouble and temptation.

On beds and books

Here's a final word on rooms: Beds can serve many purposes, but studying is not always one of them. On this, we'll bow a little bit to the psychologists who warn, "If you study on your bed, you may develop trouble sleeping; if you sleep well in bed, you may find it hard to study there because, as you relax, you'll be inclined to get sleepy." —That's what the psychologists say. Take it for what you think it's worth.

Of course, if you can both study and sleep adequately on or in bed, by all means why not? But if you can't, then study elsewhere.

The old-fashioned advice says a student should sit up straight at a desk, maintain rigid posture—shoulders back, chest out, breathe deeply . . .

We say: Assume any configuration you want, so long as you're comfortable and able to stay alert—whether it's lying on a rock, standing on your head or slouching on a couch.

CHAPTER 14

Enjoy Yourself

Live it up a little when you're in college! Grinding away at
the books, day after day, can become a real drag. That grind,
which sometimes puts cobwebs in the brain, should be broken
every now and then with a little honest recreation and
relaxation.

Historically, recreation has been recognized as a vital and
enjoyable human activity. By definition, it is a restoring or
refreshing activity — a re-creating. It is something which breaks
the monotonous drag and bolsters the spirit.

The highest grade-getters who contributed information for
this guide were very emphatic in stressing a desire to mention
recreation. One pursued an active dating life; the other was a
skier. Both feel their outside activities contributed to their
success in college. Said one, "When I study, I don't let myself think about the things I'd rather be doing. I just work
like hell. When I play, I completely forget school." Both
thought that their respective "hobbies" were mentally refreshing and helped break the boredom of study. And, both stressed
separating the two activities—studying and re-creating.

All contributors agreed on this. To half study and half goof
off is to short-change yourself on studying *and* recreation.

Separate the two and give each your full attention. There's
an old saying, "A man who drives with one arm around his
girl and the other on the wheel is not giving enough attention

to either." Apply this to college. Make sure you study and play, but keep the two activities separated.

Flying clubs and sewing clubs

The extracurricular activities offered at most colleges and universities provide a basic springboard to recreation. They are geared to a basically academic atmosphere, yet serve to satisfy the student's recreational and social needs.

Through college-sponsored activities, students are given an opportunity to develop new interests and hobbies, pursue old ones, and to meet new people and make new friends. Frequently, college-oriented clubs are subsidized by the college or church and other groups and offer students special services, facilities and activities at greatly reduced cost.

Larger universities are able to offer a greater variety of extracurricular activities, of course. But nearly all colleges have both general and special interest clubs. Sometimes the variety and opportunities are surprising.

A quick way to get an idea of what organized extracurricular activities are available at a college or university is to look through a student handbook or an annual yearbook. Student handbooks usually outline the scope of activities within a particular club, give the times the group meets, and indicate the amount of spare time a student will have to devote in order to participate fully in the activity. These handbooks can also give students an idea of the costs involved in joining a particular club, as well as a thorough rundown of the activities.

The list of recreational activities available at colleges across the U.S. is almost endless. Colleges may have clubs which specialize in flying, skiing, scuba diving, horseback riding, swimming, boating, sailing, dancing, judo, hiking, nature study and even sewing. The list is virtually endless. And you don't have to be an expert in order to join most college clubs. With the assistance of the more skilled members and frequently club instructors, students can learn new sports and activities that they might never learn in other spheres of adult life.

A flying club at one university, for example, recently boasted that 22 students had learned how to fly an airplane from scratch and had soloed in one year of club operation. Seven of these students were girls. It was interesting to note that the flying club furnished free ground training, such as navigation and weather recognition, and that a plane and qualified instructor were provided at about one third of the normal cost.

Regular club activities included taking tours of nearby airport control towers and weather stations and rebuilding antique airplanes. Three or four times during the year, the club would hold a dance or picnic.

New people, new interests

Joining a college flying club may not be your cup of tea. But mention of it may serve as an indication of the surprising variety of organized activities available to college students. Each club offers you an opportunity to meet new people, develop new interests and hobbies and to get together with people who share your particular interests.

The geographic location of each college and university offers students a chance to learn and enjoy pursuits associated with that particular locale. A college located in or near a mountainous area, for example, will probably have a large and enthusiastic ski club. Those in coastal areas or near lakes will probably have a variety of clubs oriented toward aquatic activity, such as swimming, boating, sailing and water skiing, and maybe even a club whose members are interested in marine biology. Frequently, the most popular clubs—those with the largest memberships—are the ones sponsoring activities most popular in that geographic location. An example is ski clubs.

Slaloms from the sidelines

Many students join these clubs for strictly social reasons and couldn't care less about the activity itself. Sometimes the antics of students in these clubs are hilarious. One contributor, for example, belonged to a ski club for four years and skiied only once. Most of her "ski trips" were spent pursuing other interests: men. She said about half the members of the huge college ski club were non-skiers who enjoyed the sideline participation. The club jovially welcomed their membership. The more the merrier was evidently the philosophy.

Colleges which are not ideally situated for a currently popular activity are often nevertheless able to maintain active clubs which sponsor supervised weekend and vacation-time trips to distant lakes, mountains, lodges and riding stables, at student prices.

An endless list

In many universities, especially the larger ones, there are usually such a multitude and variety of organized student activities and clubs that a student could graduate without ever hearing of some. A check of the student activities office, campus newspaper and bulletin boards in the student center will usually be enlightening.

For the athletic student who is not on a varsity team and even those who just like to throw a ball around once in a while, most campuses sponsor some form of organized intramural sports. In addition to the major sports, intramurals offer such activities as water polo, bowling, tennis, and even track events.

Most of the contributors of this material feel that athletic or physical activity of some form is essential. Athletics provide a good outlet for energies that often build up along with blisters on the backside during a heavy study schedule. Physical activity has been regarded as an essential ingredient for a healthy body and mind. Colleges recognize the need for physical activity and many require students to take physical education for at least one year.

Beyond the strictly social and athletic organizations on campus are religious groups, service organizations, the professional and honorary fraternities and academically oriented clubs.

Students usually become acquainted with religious organizations on the campuses through nearby churches. Service organizations usually conduct recruiting campaigns and initiate contact with the individual student or advertise through posters on billboards. The latter groups perform services such as ushering at football games, supervising local Boy Scout activities and assisting with or sponsoring campus events.

Academic organizations

Professional fraternities and societies are oriented toward a particular field of study, such as engineering, art, journalism, etc. They should not be confused with social fraternities, which are discussed in a separate chapter. Professional societies have undergraduate chapters for the students and graduate chapters for the man or woman working in that field. The undergraduate chapters bring together students with a particular vocational interest or inclination and the activities are usually aimed at enhancing student interest in and knowledge of that field. Many, for example, will bring in speakers who are highly experienced or expert in one or more phases of that vocation.

By the time a student comes in contact with the professional societies (usually after he has started majoring in a particular field) he generally has a pretty fair idea of their activities and knows whether he wants to join.

Students sometimes find membership in a professional fraternity or society helpful. In addition to supplementing their knowledge of an occupational or educational field, joining reflects an interest in a chosen major or career. Frequently, faculty members participate in or arrange programs.

Academically oriented clubs may be similar to the professional fraternities and societies. But they are usually open to any interested student, regardless of his major. Examples are mathematics clubs, philosophy clubs, literature clubs, French clubs, etc. They may be nationally affiliated or strictly local, and are apt to have a variety of names.

Good associations, good looks

Here again, faculty members may take an active role in the organization, and because of the association with interested

students and faculty members, some students find memberships in these academic clubs helpful. For example, a student
who is taking two years of a foreign language, such as French,
might find both direct and indirect benefits from joining the
campus French Club. Of course, no one can promise you'll
get higher grades from joining *any* extracurricular group, but
joining a specialized academic or professional organization can
boost your interest in that subject and demonstrate your motivation.

The strictly honorary fraternities or societies and clubs come
in every size and shape and are quite diverse. Some require
very little participation on the part of the student, and exist
solely to confer recognition upon the grade-getters.

Others may operate as full-scale social organizations and
hold seasonal dances, conduct fund drives for charities or
sponsor some all-campus events.

Most honoraries are segregated, in that they draw the best
students from particular groups, such as the sophomore class,
women juniors, chemistry majors, women journalism students,
or some other well-defined and limited category.

Don't spread your time too thinly

One problem frequently encountered by college students—
especially freshmen—stems from getting involved with too
many extracurricular activities.

Students who become accustomed in high school to participating in several extracurricular activities get to college, join
five or six campus organizations and then find that their time
is spread so thinly that their studies suffer. The results are especially disastrous when students take leadership positions and
committee assignments in several groups simultaneously. Some
students are capable of loading up with outside activities while
still maintaining good grades. Frequently, such students are
referred to as "pacesetters," and are capable of handling great
loads of work in a limited period of time. But most students
cannot adequately maintain their grades and also participate
in a myriad of extracurricular activities.

On many campuses, students find more pressure exerted on them to participate in outside activities than they do to study. In order to survive, college clubs and societies must recruit members and depend upon active and enthusiastic participation by members. Often, students are prodded more in their extracurricular activities than they are in the classroom.

An instructor, for example, may not care whether you show up for class, take exams, turn in assignments or even pass the course. His job is to teach those who want to learn. He will not beg his students to study or attend classes.

On the other hand, extracurricular groups often put intense pressure on members to get them to participate in scheduled activities. Persuasion may vary from a reminder telephone call where the student is put on the spot with the question, "You'll be at tomorrow's meeting, won't you?" to a system of fines or the threat of expulsion for non-attendance. True, some clubs couldn't care less whether you attend an activity; but most employ some system of coaxing members to participate regularly and actively.

Much of the pressure to participate may come from within yourself. It is a rare student who finds it more enjoyable to spend an afternoon or evening grinding away at the books than participating in an interesting outside activity he is expected to attend. The desire to socialize and recreate—or even to "party"—coupled with a little prodding by the group or your friends can present a strong case against sticking your nose in the books.

Leaders and losers

Students who achieve positions of leadership within outside groups, or who are on work committees, are under even more pressure to devote time to an activity. Some students have gotten into real academic trouble by accepting time-consuming positions of responsibility. The student business manager of the campus newspaper at one large mid-western university flunked out of school during his junior year by spending his time trying to help the floundering publication get back on its economic feet. Similarly, the president of a large fraternity in the West had to spend an extra semester in college to make up two flunked courses. He had spent a lot of time with alumni and took two extended trips to the fraternity's national head-quarters trying to secure funds for a new and larger fraternity house.

This author was personally acquainted with both students, and knew both to be academically above average prior to their "disasters."

Accepting positions of responsibility is encouraged, *provided the student is able to maintain satisfactory grades and still properly carry out the duties of his office.* If it boils down to an "either/or" situation, the student should give priority to his college studies. Two or three years hence, a record of having been president or some other officer of a large campus organization will have little significance if you don't have a college degree.

Sometimes it is hard to disappoint friends by refusing positions of trust and leadership that they offer you—or by declining to participate in some activity because of a conflict caused by your studies. But remember that your first responsibility is to *yourself.* You're there to get a degree and to make the best grades you can.

Which look best—grades or groups?

Now comes a key question: Which is more important to a prospective employer—grade-point averages or extracurricular activities?

Campus recruiters generally agree that in the fields of engineering and in the sciences, grades are given more weight. On the other hand, those looking for tomorrow's executives in the business world will pay additional attention to a student's outside activities and leadership qualities, so long as the student has a respectable overall grade average. However, the main criterion for judging a student's potential—his interest, motivation and ability—is his grade average. Unless the student has worked in the field he's majoring in, he has little else to offer a prospective employer than his academic achievement.

The best any student can offer is a *healthy combination of academic achievement and an active background in a few, selected extracurricular activities.*

Clubs can create careers

Some students have found that participation in an outside activity has sparked an interest in a recreation that they pursue long after college. Two of this author's friends actually developed careers from outside activities they stumbled into during college.

One was a geology major who became active in a campus political club. Developing an intense interest in politics, he decided to shoot for a career in it. Believing that a law degree would provide the best preparation, he changed his academic program, went on to graduate from law school, and is now a politically active practicing attorney boning up for a bid at a salaried elective office.

The other was a very bored business management major who was more interested in the flying club than in his studies. Thinking he'd rather fly than study or manage, he made some job inquiries at airline personnel offices—where he was bluntly informed that preference was given to trainee applicants who had college degrees as well as flying skills.

He got his business management degree and is now a copilot with a major airline.

CHAPTER 15

Motivation, Competition
and Money

Some constructive critics noticed this book does not carry the
overworked introduction found in so many study guides—the
"Why Go to College?" preamble.

Frankly, we didn't think we'd sell very many copies with
the old "This-Is-Why-You-Are-Here" story. And we don't
think a college student has to be told why he's in college.
We believe it's a little insulting to try to tell anyone why
he's doing whatever it is he's doing. Besides, we're not psy-
chiatrists.

Those who enroll in college and especially ones who seek
methods of succeeding probably know why they're there at
least in a general way.

An inner force and a strong back

It was suggested that we place more emphasis on that factor
which picks up when intelligence goes as far as it can—that
ingredient which is all-important to success in college and
everywhere else: Motivation.

We've referred to it frequently and our academic contributors paraphrase its meaning in a later chapter when they mention the need for determination and a strong back.

Motivation is the inner force which propels people to certain goals. In many ways it is more important than a high intelligence. A great intellectual ability which meanders, lacks direction and has no oomph behind it is a wasted gift. Like money, it can be frivolously spent, yielding no return.

Easy come—easy go

If you haven't already met a very intelligent person who squanders his brains, you will before you graduate. You'll probably meet several. Every contributor acknowledged knowing at least one such student . . . someone who superficially goes through the motions of attending college but lacks interest, ambition and a defined direction.

This author knew one student who was so brilliant that he made people around him a little uneasy. He used to amuse us with his mental gymnastics, fielding arithmetical and statistical problems with ease and slide-rule speed.

But he was well-to-do and very lazy when it came to doing —as he described it—the "dirty work" of outside assignments.

College didn't seem to challenge him and he made C's when he could have made A's without much more than a little bit of his precious play time. He quit college after two years, saying he would buy a yacht and sail to South America for kicks. He never returned.

By contrast, there are people who are not particularly brainy but who have a strong inner drive that pushes them to the limits of their abilities. There are many highly successful persons in this world who are not particularly "brainy." They deserve credit for something other than brains: Drive.

Of course, the world is not a story book. Good intentions and unlimited drive will not necessarily make a Ph.D. or physician out of a person who simply does not have the intellect to handle college material. However, millions of very average persons have attained success far beyond expectations because of strong motivation.

Motivation must come from within a person. Wise words might bring it to the surface, but no book can instill it.

What causes great deeds?

What causes motivation? Probably as many combinations of things as there are persons who possess it. Some people need prestige or recognition; others may have a desire to compensate for a real or imagined inadequacy or to perform some deed they think must be done, to win the esteem of their friends or families, to learn all they can about a subject that interests them, or merely to develop themselves to their limits. Many are motivated by a desire for money—for the sake of amassing a fortune or as a means to a comfortable life.

Some individuals appear to have been born with an aggressiveness and drive, and seem to thrive on hurdles and competition. They sense deep satisfaction from winning, from achieving.

Those motivated by a desire for money or at least a comfortable income are headed in the proper direction, statistically speaking, by going to college. Research shows that a college graduate can expect to earn somewhere between $100,-000 and a quarter of a million dollars more during his lifetime than a non-graduate. So, overlooking the prestige, the self-satisfaction and other values of a college education, you can assume that college pays off in dollars and cents.

A ticket of admission

It is true that many people have and will continue to become successful and prosperous without college diplomas. A college degree is no guarantee that the world is at your feet. Nevertheless, the stories of "from janitor to corporation president" are few these days. Somehow, the college graduate has an edge over the other man just as the technically trained craftsman has an advantage over unskilled workers. Sometimes it seems almost unfair that the college graduate gets the promotion over his equally adept colleague. But it is a fact of life.

Several years ago, a high school diploma set a wage-earner apart from others. And getting a year or two of college was a distinct accomplishment. But those days are history, and persons who doubt this are invited to compete with college graduates in seeking professional or business job opportunities and advancement. Some fields, of course, require more than a bachelor's degree.

College these days is pretty much an all-or-nothing proposition. This is especially true for men. You either have a degree or you don't.

Getting a degree is not an automatic privilege that comes with paying tuition and attending classes for four, five, or seven years. It is, for most students, a challenge which requires a great deal of time, effort and a willingness to hang on and fight.

People who thrive on competition couldn't have picked a better time to go to college.

Millions versus you

Just so you know where you stand—and what you are up against—it might be worthwhile taking a brief look at the competition. Times are getting tough, educationally speaking. In 1970, some seven million grown-up post-war babies arrived on the nation's college campuses. And it's getting worse. This figure is expected to *double* by the end of this decade, according to enrollment projections.

Thousands of students are being turned away by crowded colleges each year and thousands of others will be shown quick exits when they fail to make the grade. In one state alone, an educational survey says, some 25,000 eligible students were refused admission in a one-year period.*

Not only are there more students as a result of the baby boom that followed World War II, but the percentage of graduating seniors seeking college training is also increasing. For example, in 1950, only about 18 per cent of high school graduates went to college. In 1955, 29 per cent went on to college, and in 1965, that figure reached 43 per cent.

Through the 1970's, the percentage seeking admission to

* The Associated Press.

college is expected to go even higher. While colleges and universities across the country are engaged in crash building programs, they are not able to keep up with this boom and are bulging at their seams, so to speak.

Tough to get in—tougher to stay in

Crowded institutions have reached a point where they simply do not have enough room for those students not serious about learning. Not only must students compete for entrance into college; they must compete to *stay* in.

The party-going college student, the disinterested youth, those who are physically present on campus because their parents want them to go to school, and the girl whose primary objective is to meet as many potential husbands as she can, are now finding short-lived college careers. And unfortunately for so many of these people, having merely attended college means little when it comes to getting a job.

Undergraduates planning to do graduate work also face tough competition, and college grades are a prime factor when applying for a graduate program. In 1950, less than one in ten bachelor's degree holders enrolled in graduate school. In the 1960's, more than one in four graduates went on to advanced college programs.

College is a big, tough business, and the historic days of leisurely sitting under a tree reflecting on higher thoughts are over.

CHAPTER 16

Watch Your Grades Soar

You've probably heard the cliché about this country's great millionaires of the 19th century: The first million was the hardest to earn; the successive millions came easily.

Money makes money. Nothing succeeds like success. These are all trite yet interesting phrases because they're generally true. The same axioms hold in college. Once a student starts racking up good grades, he has a solid foot in the door for continued academic success. There is probably a variety of reasons for this. Here are two: Reputations, like first impressions, have a way of sticking. The word somehow gets around that certain students are workers—that they're grade-earners. Sometimes it is evident from a student's approach to a class that he's a high-scorer.

Getting out of the woods

Secondly, it is a case of developing the ability to do well. Once you've managed to find your way to a hard-to-reach place, you find it's easier to get there a second, third or fourth time. We learn shortcuts and we learn from our mistakes.

Frequently, you'll see students who knock themselves out at first to make high grades. Later, they slack off a little yet are still able to maintain high grades. For them, the phrase "once an A student, always an A student" seems to hold true.

This may sound like a lot of jibberish, but what it boils

down to is this: Somehow, the high-scorers have found their own methods for making good grades. Through experience—in high school or college—they learned to recognize what is expected of them and formulated their own techniques. They know the shortcuts. Many of the tips outlined in this book are second nature to these habitually good students who have developed—through practice—good, efficient study habits. Often, their affinity for academic success is nothing more than the fact that *they have had practice doing well.*

Profits from losses

During your stay in college, try to profit from your mistakes. Some optimists say we learn the most from our mistakes. Well, maybe we do if we don't give up first. At any rate, your academic mistakes and shortcomings can be salvaged and turned into something of value when they are clearly pointed out and if you try to look at them objectively. If you are unable to see clearly your mistakes and shortcomings, or cannot ascertain the problem through a little thinking or analysis, talk with members of your faculty. Don't be argumentative when you make your inquiries. Sometimes students are sensitive to criticism and react aggressively and defensively when instructors point out faults. Accept constructive criticism gratefully. Part of a teacher's job is to correct; only by accepting his criticism can you learn and improve.

Remember that instructors are different. An A to one instructor might rate only a C with another, and vice versa. Some are more concerned with proper procedure than with exact answers; others look only at answers. Try, through your own experiences and mistakes, to determine each instructor's preferences and your own shortcomings.

Set your own schedule

Now we'll consider a topic which has been omitted previously from this book—one which is usually discussed in detail in the traditional study guides: How much time should you spend studying? This is something which only you can prescribe. Obviously, the need will vary with each individual and each course. Some students are able to breeze through a course while others in the same class will have to sweat and labor for every point.

Traditionally, students are advised to spend two hours studying for each hour of classroom instruction. This is a sort of rule-of-thumb offered in many colleges and in numerous study guides. We think it is ridiculous. You may encounter some courses where you'll have to spend more than this arbitrarily suggested two hours. And you'll probably have many courses which require much less time.

Most students taking full loads find it difficult, if not impossible, to spend two hours in outside study for every hour in the classroom. Hence, they must develop techniques for making the most efficient use of their study effort.

This book contains many such time-saving techniques. They've all been tested and used successfully. The contributors, as explained in prefacing remarks, are all recent college graduates. We're from different schools and we majored in different subjects ranging from the engineering fields to fine arts. And, we have a pretty broad span of overall averages.

Who falls behind is lost

At one extreme was a student who had a D average after two years of college. He took a little vacation and was readmitted on a probationary status some time later. Somewhere along the line he "got smart," found a good groove in his second go-around, and maintained a high B average during his last two years. He looked back with regret on his first two years. His two years of D's had so damaged his cumulative effort that he barely made a C overall average despite his fine showing during his junior and senior years. He graduated offering this advice: "He who gets behind is lost." His experience shows that a poor start can mean a mediocre finish no matter how hard you run after you pick yourself up.

At the other extreme were students who graduated with highest honors. One offers an interesting history. For three years, she spent almost every minute of her time studying. She even turned down many weekend dates and carried few outside activities because of the academic demands of college. Then she discovered ways to improve her efficiency. She started enjoying an active social life, spent a little less time with the books, and made even better grades.

Spot them and use them

Several other contributors had similar experiences. The reason is simply that they learned ideas and techniques which are presented here—tips based not on speculation or research, but on first-hand experience. These tips provided an easier way to better grades.

Find those which will help you and begin putting them to use. Stay alert for other ideas and seek legitimate shortcuts of your own. Glance through this book occasionally. You'll find easier ways to better grades.

CHAPTER 17

A Little Extra Cash

What is it that college students seldom have enough of and could always use a little more of—something with which they are frequently preoccupied?

Among other things, it's money.

From the high-living student who writes to his wealthy father every month to those who must support families while trying to get an education, there is a deep concern for money.

A college student's earning potential is usually low, yet his expenses—even if he leads a relatively austere life—can be fantastic. Tuition or student fees, rent and food, books, clothing and social delights are expensive. The student whose parents are able to subsidize fully his or her education is lucky; those who have tucked away ample bankrolls for their own educations are few.

Some have to support wives, pay for babies, and meet college expenses without a cent of outside help. Many support themselves in part and get limited help from relatives who can spare a few dollars now and then.

Free money—yours by asking

If you're in a financial bind or find it tough meeting your expenses, you might look for a scholarship as a partial solution.

"Who, ME?" you may ask. "Yes, YOU" is our answer. Here's why:

Every year, hundreds of thousands of scholarship dollars sit idle because no serious students applied for the funds.

There was a time when scholarships were few. They were grants to the very brilliant but impoverished students who showed great potential. This isn't quite so any more. Thousands of scholarships are available to average but sincere students who are in need or who would even make good use of financial assistance while going to or continuing college.

$$$ for C's

You do not necessarily have to boast an A or even a high B average in order to qualify for some of the available scholarships. A satisfactory grade average, an interest in college and a financial need are all that are required for many grants.

Scholarships may be worth anywhere from a few bucks to several thousand dollars a year. Some are straight cash grants handed out with a letter saying: "Here you are, congratulations, good luck." Others have some strings attached. At one university, a "strings-attached" scholarship requires only that the student have a C average, a financial need and a desire to continue college. But it stipulates the student be of "exceptional character." Among the benefactor's definitions of "exceptional character" are requirements that the recipient be a non-drinker and a non-smoker.

Many students would be ineligible or otherwise uninterested in this grant. The university where this grant was awarded once announced—much to the tongue-in-cheek delight of newspapers across the country—that the scholarship was idle for five years in a row.

Other strings-attached grants are less socially restrictive but require the student to pledge he will work at least one year in a given occupation. These scholarships are usually awarded to juniors and seniors who have shown an interest in a particular major favored by the benefactor, such as engineering, pharmacy, law and medicine, education or journalism.

The mutual aid "bribe"

Sometimes companies seeking prospective career employees offer special deals which combine scholarships or loans with summer jobs.

An engineering student and friend of this author took a summer job with a large scientific research firm after his freshman year. The company provided a good summer internship program at good wages and offered "loans" toward college costs. Time spent with the company during summers was credited toward his starting salary upon graduation, and each year he participated in the program counted as one full year toward retirement, longevity and seniority benefits.

The "loan" was considered paid in full when he went to work full time after graduating. Had he chosen to work elsewhere, he would have been expected to repay the loan at no interest and at his convenience, within reason.

Some students might object to this program, saying that the recipient is selling himself to a big business or is committing himself too far in advance. However, this student found it a way to finance an education, get good summer training with pay and a career job offer at an above-average salary upon graduating.

Scholarships and loans, both with and without obligatory clauses, are there for the asking. Of course, some are highly competitive on a nation-wide basis. Others are restricted to students in one department in a particular college or university. Sponsors range from huge, world-wide corporations or labor unions to veterans' organizations, high school and college alumni groups, local civic groups, merchants and well-to-do individuals.

Hunt for money

The reason so many scholarships and student loans go begging is that few students know about them. They are not promoted or advertised in newspapers, but are there only for those interested and needy enough to seek them out.

One contributor picked up a tuition scholarship during his senior year, despite his mediocre grade average, for one simple reason: He was the *only applicant* and he needed money. His instructors, when asked for references, reported only that he was an average student, did what was expected and would probably graduate.

Some scholarships require proof of need

A few scholarships require the applicant to give documented proof of his financial need by stating his parents' occupations, salaries, savings account balances, number of dependents and other personal information. And occasionally, applicants or their parents object to providing the information or to subjecting themselves to a financial investigation, calling it an invasion of privacy.

It *is* an invasion, inasmuch as personal finances are usually matters that people prefer to keep to themselves. People volunteer this information all the time when seeking credit; but the goals are different and a credit applicant is trying to prove he is financially stable and able to meet the obligations of a loan. Somehow, when it comes to scholarships, people are more reluctant or resentful about personal finances. Pride is at stake because, in our society, money is so often used as a yardstick to measure success. One can hardly blame a father for resenting a questionnaire in which he is, in effect, expected to prove he is poor or otherwise incapable of helping his children go to college.

On the other hand, benefactors with sincere desires to assist the needy cannot be criticized for an inquisitive attitude. They want assurance that their money is being spent where it is needed most. They want their hundreds or thousands of dollars to go to students who might not otherwise be able to go to college—and not to those whose parents are perfectly able to pay the freight themselves.

This raises a question which always affects a handful of students: How do they get such scholarships if they are totally without parental help yet have parents who could afford to pay college expenses?

Some affluent parents, for a variety of reasons, believe in "kicking the young 'uns outta the nest" when they graduate from high school or reach a certain age. And sometimes, a child from a broken home will lose his dependency allotment at college age—when an estranged father is no longer required to provide for him.

Some sponsors of scholarships intended for the most needy students will take this into account; others flatly reject applicants whose parents have money.

Some disregard finances

Nowadays, however, there are thousands of scholarships which do not delve deeply into finances. Their application forms ask only, "Would your education benefit from financial assistance?" Others make absolutely no reference to a student's monetary resources and are based solely on other criteria, such as the results of a test or interview, contest or past performance.

Still other scholarships, while competitive, are awarded to students with a particular background or whose parent might be one of the following:

—Employed in a specific vocation.
—Employee of the sponsoring company.
—Deceased employee of sponsor.
—Deceased peace officer.
—A veteran (and some specify branch of service).
—Deceased or disabled veteran.
—Member of a labor organization (varying from an international union to a specific local).

Some, based on the applicant alone, list one of the following as a requisite:

—Veteran.
—Practicing member of a particular faith.
—Member of a specified ethnic or racial group.

—Descendant of a Revolutionary or Civil War veteran.

—A worker who has demonstrated potential in his field.

—A first generation American whose parents were born in a specified foreign country.

—Performance of a heroic act.

—Outstanding contribution to a community or society in general.

A guide to scholarships

The subject of scholarships fills entire volumes, and those interested in specific details of what's available, where, how to apply and even *how to compete* are urged to read one of the several books available on the subject. In general, these books outline scholarships available, the requirements for each, discuss loans and other grants and some even contain review material for preparing for competitive scholarship exams.

Loans offer alternatives

In addition to scholarships, there are numerous loans available for students who need funds. Many firms and agencies, including the federal and state governments, offer low- or no-interest loans with little or no collateral required. Unlike scholarships, these are not pure gifts. They are loans in the strictest business sense and enable a student to enroll in or finish college and then arrange a reasonable repayment program upon graduating and finding a job. A college or bank official can advise you on these.

Working your way through college

Another alternative solution to financial problems—for the student not already employed—is a full or part time job.

Part time jobs involving a few hours a week or perhaps one day each weekend are especially helpful to those who need just a few extra dollars to make ends meet.

Most colleges have student employment centers which keep

tabs on full and part time job prospects both at the college and in the surrounding community.

Jobs specifically for students

Colleges frequently hire their own students to augment regular secretarial and clerical staffs, maintenance departments, on-campus sales departments (bookstores, playhouses, cafeterias, etc.) and laboratory staffs.

Student domiciles (dormitories, boarding houses, apartments) frequently offer room and board free or at reduced rates to students who handle maintenance, clerical or kitchen tasks. Dining room helpers in most student chow halls earn their meals.

Firms in college communities seek students for part-time weekend and evening relief work. Among the many full and part time jobs filled by college students are those of gas station attendants, bus and taxi drivers, movie ticket vendors, domestic workers and gardeners at private homes, stock and sales clerks, short-order cooks, waiters, bartenders, PBX operators, custodians, campus sales representatives, counter check-out clerks, office assistants, stenographers, classified ad takers on local and campus newspapers, dishwashers, factory workers and so on.

In addition to student employment centers, of course, are the customary channels for getting a job—newspaper help-wanted ads and personal visits to local businesses.

Some firms prefer to hire students who drop in on their own volition, rather than to interview a parade of students sent down by the campus employment centers.

Local county and city recreation departments offer good work prospects, as many seek college-age persons to supervise sports and crafts programs. Duties can range from merely keeping kiddies out of playground fights and coaching or refereeing sports to taking kids on overnight hikes.

Students with lifesaving or swimming instructor certificates can almost always get jobs at nearby public and private pools and beaches.

Glamor and good wages come later

Few jobs available to college students are glamorous or high paying. But they offer at least a minimum wage and enable students to pay their bills. Sometimes the drag of a dull, dead-end temporary job even provides a solid, motivating kick in the rear end when the academics get rough. One contributor who performed a very dull and monotonous job on an assembly line night shift credited the horrible monotony with providing the greatest single incentive for going to college and getting his degree.

"The thought of spending years, or a lifetime, doing that same thing night after night was just too much. That's when I decided to go to school," he said.

Additional benefits

Having worked while in college offers you an extra laurel in seeking a job after graduation. Employers are always interested in knowing whether applicants worked at outside jobs. Most application forms ask specifically whether the student worked. If he did, he may be asked to list former employers and the percentage of college expenses he earned. The theory seems to be that the student who had to work has demonstrated additional ambition, responsibility and serious concern for his future.

Those employers who examine a graduate's grades make considerable concessions to those who have found it necessary or desirable to hold jobs in college. The author is not suggesting that students with lower grades take jobs as excuses, but it is worth noting the interest given to a prior work record.

Some are sympathetic

The same reaction has been noted in instructors—and this is again another reason for making personal contact. If you're working several hours a week earning money for college expenses, let it be known . . . in a subtle fashion. Instructors with sympathetic attitudes may take this into account.

Don't make a big issue of it, though, or press for special favors on the grounds that you are the poor victim of a sweatshop. Let *the instructor* take the initiative of giving special consideration to your circumstances, if he has the inclination. Everyone prefers to give of his own free will—to see himself as a warm, understanding human—rather than to be solicited head-on for special favors.

Students with outside jobs are advised against using the job as an excuse for missing a class, test or assignment, except in very unusual circumstances. Most firms augmenting their labor forces with college students are aware that the student's prime interest is his schooling. Usually they are willing to make an occasional adjustment in a student-worker's schedule to accommodate academic demands.

Can you work in your field?

In seeking an outside job, it is most advantageous if a student can find something related to his ultimate professional field. Besides the money it provides during college, the experience and training may pay off both during and after college.

It puts you in contact with the subjects you are studying and sometimes gives you a chance to *apply* your learning and thereby increase your understanding and familiarity with things you deal with in the classroom. If other employees are graduates in the field you are studying, you can profit from their assistance and knowledge.

Working in a professionally related field boosts your value when you graduate. You will have had *working experience* in that area. With it you may be in a position to win out over competing applicants, command a better job offer and even a higher starting salary.

Building valuable experience

One contributor worked an average of 20 hours as an apprentice during the school year and full time during summers before his junior and senior years. After graduating, he took a job with another company and was credited with a flat 18 months' experience—enough to start him at a salary of $135 a month more than other new graduates earned.

He said that his instructors were impressed by the fact he was interested enough in the field to pursue it outside the classroom. He was also able to cite practical applications of theory in his examinations, giving him a distinct edge over the other students.

Among the many examples of academic majors and related jobs they can seek are:

—Electrical engineering students working in electronics labs and even radio repair shops.

—Sales, advertising or marketing majors in direct sales work.

—Journalism students working on local newspapers.

—Accounting majors who do bookkeeping.

—Civil engineering students who do construction and surveying jobs.

—Pharmacy students assisting in drug stores.

Good, related experiences

If you can't get a job related to your academic specialty, yet have some choice of openings available, pick something that will not become horribly tedious or exhausting and one which can give you *some* useful experience, backgrounding or *associations*.

If your career will involve coming in contact with clients or people in general, seek a part time job where you'll be dealing with people. If you major in English, literature, education, law, history or the arts, you'd probably get more from working in a book store than, for example, stocking merchandise in a shoe store.

This is common sense, and there's no need to explain the why's. Naturally, wages are an important factor in job selection too. But if you can forgo a slightly higher salary for a more interesting or beneficial part time or temporary job, take the latter. Some jobs, where a student is merely "standing by," allow him time to study.

One other prospect worth mentioning is that of working in the department where you are majoring. One contributor was acquainted with a chemistry major who spent three years cleaning labs in the chemistry building. What better way to get personally acquainted with the department staff—and maybe get a little extra coaching on the side?

Work, study or both?

Students who are pretty much left to their own financial resources often come to grips with the question of whether to go to school and work simultaneously or to alternate the two. It is impossible to offer a flat answer.

Some young people possess extraordinary abilities and energy and are able to take a normal college load while holding down a full time job. Many who try this double life, however, meet with disaster and the wearing of two hats takes its toll—in grades and health.

Organizations sponsoring loans and scholarships have become aware of this either-way-you-lose problem. Hence, students in this situation are especially encouraged to seek financial assistance.

If possible, hang on

Any way you can stay in school without jeopardizing your health or your grades is the best bet, even if it means going to night school, extension school or taking accredited correspondence courses. Whenever a student drops out of school —for work or any other reason—he risks running into obstacles which may delay or totally prevent his return.

There is also a rustiness factor. A student loses some of his studying ability, work habits and disciplines, and intellectual alertness during an extended break. Three contributors whose schooling was interrupted for lengthy periods agree it is difficult getting back into the groove.

Budget your money

Managing finances is out of this book's scope, but we suggest that students facing financial problems keep a tight reign on their expenses. To most students pressed for money, this advice sounds unnecessary—yet a lot of people insist on doing things in high style or not at all. In a college environment there are many costly temptations, and it takes real self-discipline to stay within a limited and long-range income-expense budget.

One student with whom this author was acquainted won a substantial cash scholarship to any school of his choice. He picked a distant, top-notch and expensive private institution. He received no parental help and was embarrassed about his background of relative poverty. Working half time, he played an artificial role in school. He bought a nearly new prestige car on extended credit terms; outfitted himself with an elaborate wardrobe, also bought on credit; rented an expensive off-campus apartment; purchased an electric typewriter, television set and a high quality FM-phonograph stereo combination; wined and dined his dates in first class establishments—and dropped out of school after a year and a half because he couldn't pay his fourth semester tuition. His car was repossessed and he wound up in a debtor's court.

Had he settled for a lower-cost state college, conservative spending habits and a few sacrifices, he probably could have made it to a degree.

He can't be criticized for the way he spent his own money (although the scholarship sponsor probably was not very pleased), but he certainly can be cited as an example of someone who exchanged an education for the privilege of temporary social status and the high life. Probably more common are students who lead grandiose school lives on funds provided by parents who make sizable sacrifices to send their children to college.

If you have to forego some of the social joys in order to

stretch the money and hang in until graduation, make the sacrifice, tighten your belt and settle for standing room only. College is really a pretty short period of adult life and probably the most important. Those forced to go without during college will be able to make up for it in later years.

A word of caution to job seekers

Students seeking jobs should be cautious about one work field.

Probably the most highly promoted college student position and the hardest to regulate by campus and governmental authorities is the campus representative or sales agent.

Student representatives are always being sought—through newspaper ads and billboards and by fast-talking distributors who draw names from student employment agency registrations, mailing lists and residence directories.

The big promotional pitch given this work and the set-your-own-work-schedule angle are great lures to students seeking income. Since so many students are solicited for these campus representative jobs, it might be worth a quick discussion. Also, little has been published to guide students in these matters.

The immediate disadvantage in working as a commissioned campus sales representative is that there is seldom a guaranteed wage for hours worked. Payment is entirely contingent upon the amount of business a representative can solicit. A student could spend hundreds of hours getting little or no return for his effort, time and expense.

Easy money? Very unlikely

Be cautious about contracting to serve as "campus rep" for firms which make extraordinary promises.

Despite legislation, there are always unscrupulous fly-by-night organizations which exploit the naive and needy—and college students seem to be regarded as prime targets.

There are numerous instances on record where unsuspecting students have been roped into contracts where they have aided some company without making one thin dime for their own hard work. On top of that, if a firm fails to furnish the buyer with the product or service that you as the agent sell, you may be held liable.

Danger signals

Be careful about firms which:

—Require you to make the sale but instruct the buyer to send his money directly to the company.

—Require you to pay a sizable deposit on a sales kit.

—Carry a clause in your contract saying that your commission will be paid only after each group of sales, such as 50 sales.

—Sell products of questionable quality or with which you are unfamiliar.

—Penalize you financially for not making a quota.

—Promise you tremendous profits or commissions—("Average $150 a week in just 10 hours' spare time" etc.).

—Offer glamorous and expensive rewards for making quotas.

—Offer exclusive territories which may not be exclusive at all.

—Suggest that the campus will beat a path to your door to obtain this wonderful product or service.

—Ask you to do anything which appears unethical or downright illegal.

—Require a considerable investment to get into a temporary business.

—Display corny endorsements and testimonials from obscure, so-called satisified sales agents or customers.

—Require advance payments for wholesale quantities of merchandise which you may not be able to sell.

—Do not readily identify themselves or their products to inquiring applicants.

—List only a postal box address.

—Have developed a questionable reputation.

Having some of these characteristics does not necessarily

mean an outfit is a phony. But firms exhibiting any of these warrant further checking.

Many are legit

Certainly there are many legitimate, well-established and reputable businesses which sell through campus representatives. There are good firms selling all kinds of merchandise— from magazine subscriptions to campus jewelry, personalized stationery and greeting cards. Many aggressive, hard-working college students have been able to earn a substantial amount of money in campus sales work. One enterprising student at a state university walked into a freshman dormitory one fall night taking orders for collegiate sweatshirts bearing the school's name. He left two hours later with about $150 in commissions.

If you doubt the credibility of a firm, check with campus authorities and the local police, Better Business Bureau and chamber of commerce, where records of complaint would be kept on file. These agencies can also tell you whether soliciting is prohibited or requires a license.

If there is no record of any kind—either good or bad— and you still have doubts, drop a postcard to the business bureau or chamber of commerce in the city where the firm is headquartered, asking them about the firm.

The G.I. bill

The federal government makes special funds available to veterans of the armed forces. The G.I. Bill has been instituted for those who have served on active duty since the beginning of the Second World War. While the "Bill" has periodically been discontinued between conflicts, it has been renewed with each new involvement and was again instituted in the Vietnam conflict. GIs usually know whether they're eligible. A veterans' affairs advisor on college campuses or any Veterans' Administration office can advise a student on his eligibility and benefits.

CHAPTER **18**

Fraternities, Sororities, Grades and You

The question of whether to join a social fraternity or sorority is an important matter to many new college students. And those who do plan to join a fraternal organization are confronted with still another decision: which one?

Since both fraternities and sororities are social, fraternal organizations, the term "fraternity" here will apply to both.

Some students know in advance whether they plan to join a social fraternity and many even know which ones they intend to pledge. This is especially true of those who have lived near their colleges or have friends or relatives who have cut a path for them. But for the student who does not know whether to join nor which one, a lot of serious thinking and looking is required.

Most social fraternities—those which own houses and form a tightly knit social system—place a number of demands upon the student and will become an important part of his or her college life. It is therefore wise to take a good, long look before making a commitment.

Rush week

Unfortunately, the "Greek" systems at many universities and colleges subject freshmen to a pre-school "rush week" which is just that. The student becomes rapidly acquainted with several fraternities during a short time and sees them at their best. They look at him and he looks at them. If a fraternity likes an individual, he is offered a bid. When the student accepts the most attractive bid, he becomes a pledge. Pledgeship periods usually are one quarter or one semester long, and are much like an engagement. Each takes a close look at the other and arrives at a final decision.

Assuming there is no serious discord and the student makes the required grades, he is initiated. The initiation marks the permanent bind and is like the marriage. After initiation, the student and fraternity are pretty much stuck with the choice—at least during an undergraduate career at that institution.

Social fraternities are so varied that it would be impossible to discuss all types at length. There are independent fraternal groups located on just one particular campus and there are huge nationally organized fraternities which own houses on more than a hundred campuses across the country and even maintain active alumni chapters. Here, we will discuss the national fraternal system.

The system is changing

The fraternal system, in general, has undergone considerable modification during the past two decades. Once regarded as posh lodges for the well-to-do students, fraternities have become more of an "any student's" organization. Most students who are comfortably able to afford college can afford to belong to a fraternity.

With the changes in attitude and pressures toward civil rights, fraternities have achieved a greater degree of local autonomy—primarily because it was forced upon them. Those major fraternities which once had restrictive membership clauses have for the most part removed them and have granted individual chapters the permission to decide on their own members without reference to ethnic or religious background and without review by a higher authority. The notorious

"Hell Weeks" generally have also been de-emphasized.

Ten years ago, it was not an unusual sight to see an initiation candidate running around campus during "Hell Week" with a plunger attached to the top of his head. He'd carry a dime-store "ray gun" which he'd point at attractive coeds and say "zap, zap."

Over the past few years, however, many colleges have absolutely forbidden the traditional "Hell Week" harassment, and a new term, "Help Week," was coined. Candidates for initiation, instead of spending all their time doing antics, have been used for constructive work projects either in the fraternity house itself or on the campus.

Many colleges are doing away with the whirlwind rush weeks in favor of an "open rush" program which enables students to take longer both looking at fraternities and deciding which if any to join. But the rush week programs at the outset of each term are still prevalent.

Look at the local chapter

When you are looking at fraternities, keep your eye on the *local chapter*. Some fraternities will boast about the huge number of chapters across the country and the thousands of persons who have joined since the organization was founded. The fraternity's national reputation may be excellent. Remember, though, that most of your association with a fraternity will be with one particular chapter. It is fine for students to join a house because of the prestige the fraternity enjoys nationally. However, the relationship between the student and his fellow "brothers" in that house is—in our opinion—more important than national reputation.

Besides, the national fraternities all have "good" and "poor" houses. Almost any fraternity official will concede that his organization has some "problem" chapters.

See beyond the varnish

Students being "rushed" by a fraternity should keep in mind that houses and members are usually at their best when they are recruiting. Beware of promises of greatness where greatness does not exist. A classic example of the gilded fraternity house was observed recently on the campus of a large state university. The fraternity members pointed to an empty lot next door where a bulldozer had plowed up a little earth. They explained, "We just broke ground for our new house. It should be completed within a year."

For three years, the fraternity kept up the ruse by renting a bulldozer every rush week—until that and other less-than-ethical operations resulted in the chapter's suspension.

Look at the younger members of the fraternity when you "rush." These are the ones with whom you will be living and associating. When you're in the final invited-back stages of rushing, take a look at your fellow rushees and decide whether they are people you want to associate with for four years.

Most college graduates who were members of fraternities or sororities will tell you that finding a group in which you can get along harmoniously is the most important consideration.

Ask questions when you rush

If you're rushing several fraternities, plan to ask a lot of questions about each. One very fair—and often enlightening —question concerns the chapter's grade average and academic standing. Every local chapter of every social fraternity will compute an average grade for the active members. If a fraternity's grade average and academic standing on the campus are below average or poor, watch out!

How much time is involved?

Find out the demands that will be made on you if you join. Will you be required to live in the fraternity house during most of your undergraduate career? Some fraternities —especially those chapters which are struggling financially— have very rigid rules on this. Others, with a membership larger than the house can adequately accommodate, may have to turn away some members, such as seniors.

You might also inquire the time demands that will be made on you, both during your pledgeship period and as an active member.

You may, as a pledge, be required to attend daily and weekend clean-up sessions at the house. As a member, you might have to attend a certain amount of "functions," parties, intramural games, etc.

Determine whether this participation will be compatible with your plans and aspirations.

And how much money?

Students concerned with their finances should pay particular attention to the costs of the fraternities they visit. The financial demands made by fraternities may vary greatly from one to another.

Questions to ask are:

What are monthly dues and do they apply to the school year or to a 12-month year? What is the cost of room and board? Does the fraternity levy special assessments, and if so, what for? How much are they and are they mandatory?

An example of a special assessment would be a flat charge to members to foot the cost of a special dance, such as a spring ball. In some houses the charge might be optional; only those who attend must pay. In other chapters, the charge might be automatic—whether or not the member participates in the activity.

Are extra charges made during or at the end of each year to balance the books or build a reserve for the next fall? Are members obligated to pay annual alumni dues after graduation? How much is the initiation fee? Are a member's parents expected to make contributions?

Whether and which

The mere listing of these questions may present the reader with a grim picture. This is not the author's intent. Rather, the intent here is to point out that membership in a fraternity obligates a student to a certain amount of time and money. It is wise for prospective members to find out in advance how much of each will be required.

Knowing about these matters beforehand will help you determine whether you want to join a fraternity and which ones are better suited to your availability and finances. And it will help you plan your other activities and expenses.

Many fraternities point to the benefits they continue to offer following graduation. These may range from membership in alumni clubs and free admission to annual homecoming parties sponsored by the local chapter—to the privilege of being able to get free or low-cost overnight accommodations at any other chapter within that national fraternity.

These benefits may be advantageous and enjoyable, but they're only garnishings. The major relationship you'll have with a fraternity will be during your undergraduate career.

Legacies and rejections

Students should be cautious about joining a particular fraternity because a family member or family friend has been a member of that chapter or national fraternity. Legacies pose an awkard situation for everyone involved—both the rushee and the fraternity. The nature of a group within a chapter can change completely in just a couple of years and the type of people in a national fraternity can vary greatly from one chapter to the next. The ties that members of your family or friends have with a particular chapter or national fraternity may be worth considering when you decide which house to join, but keep your eye on the other considerations as well.

Sometimes being a rejected legacy—or merely having his heart set on joining a particular fraternity—can be disappointing to a student who doesn't get the bid he expected or wanted. At the end of fall rush week every year, thousands of students face what they feel is humiliation and disappointment. Women students are usually more emotional about this. Maybe someone in the family was a member of Alpha Alpha Alpha and naturally, Peggy was expected to join Alpha Alpha Alpha, too. But Peggy didn't get a bid. Peggy may be so upset she doesn't even want to go on in college.

Or maybe Marilyn arrives at college thinking she simply must join Alpha Beta Gamma in order to have the prestige she wants. Same story—tears and heartbreak.

Passed over?—So what!

Of course, it is ridiculous for a student to suffer great damage to the ego because of such a situation. But it happens. Students who don't get the bid they were after should forget about it. Just as the jilted lover is consoled with the remark, "There's plenty of other fish in the ocean," the rejected rushee should realize there are plenty of other fraternities, sororities and social groups.

Failure to get a bid does not necessarily mean that the student is not considered suitable to the group. Often, in rush parties, rushees get overlooked in the large crowd and when it comes time to prepare bids, no one remembers meeting the individual. Even if this is not the case and the student is passed over for other reasons, no student should get upset about it. All it takes is for one or two members of a whole chapter to say "no" for any reason at all and a rushee can be passed over. So maybe someone didn't like the way the rushee parts his hair. So what? So forget it!

Several of the graduates who contributed information for this study guide were members of the Greek system. And most conceded that the system can be pretty snobbish. Each fraternity likes to think it is the best and strives to recruit pledges who, in the opinion of the members, seem most like themselves.

Large or small house?

Students who are bent upon joining a fraternity but have no preconceived preference face the question of whether to join a large or small house.

Many students find that smaller houses offer a closer camaraderie and that an "average" member has more of a chance to take a leadership position.

Larger houses sometimes tend to be cliquish—that is, members form tightly-knit little groups within the house. But there are a greater variety and number of people from which to choose friends.

The size of a chapter best suited to an individual will depend strictly upon his own goals.

Fraternities and grades—views differ

Now the all-important question: What is the effect of fraternity membership on a student's grades?

Opinions differ widely on this. Some say fraternity or sorority life interfered with their studies because of time demands and noise in the house during the evening hours. Others say that fraternity "study tables," coaching seminars, and the chance to live with older more experienced students helped them academically.

It's a question that even college administrators differ on and many steer clear of answering it because no matter what position they take, someone will be offended.

The situation may vary from one house to another and from one campus to another. A quick way to get an idea, of course, is to compare an individual chapter's grade average or an all-fraternity average with an all-men's, all-women's or all-students' grade average. These statistics are usually made available by the college administration, the campus newspaper, the inter-fraternity council on that campus or by each chapter.

Those chapters which have above-average grades *seldom keep it secret*. They'll probably show charts and tables to the rushee to clearly show their academic prowess.

On the other hand, chapters which are not doing so well academically will probably avoid the topic or skip over it lightly if the question is raised.

Generally speaking, membership in a fraternity will have little effect on a student's overall performance in college, in the opinion of this author. A good student who places academics first is bound to achieve good grades whether or not he's in a fraternity. A poor student—one to whom college itself is secondary to other activities—will probably miss the mark regardless.

Whether you join a fraternal organization should be strictly up to you. Make sure, if you join, that you're making a carefully considered choice of houses. There are usually many opportunities during a college career to join, should you not receive any attractive bids during your first rush experience. Don't accept a bid and pledge merely for the sake of belonging to *any* fraternity.

Open rush—a better view

During the academic year, most fraternities conduct what is known as an "open rush program." Students interested in the prospect of joining a fraternity place their names on a list, and fraternities seeking pledges will invite from that list prospective rushees over for dinner, or other occasions, in order to get acquainted.

Open rush meetings are usually more candid than rush week meetings, and are apt to be less formal. They also offer both the individual and the fraternity more time to decide matters. Some campuses permit uncommitted students to go through rush week a second time.

The binding tie

Once you've made a choice, served your pledgeship and have been initiated, the membership is virtually final. If a member becomes disenchanted with the group, it may be awkward and embarrassing to break the tie. Sometimes an unhappy member can make arrangements to dissociate with the chapter quietly—particularly in those whose membership strength is at or above par. The member moves out of the house, refrains from participating in the activities, may agree not to associate with other members and *may* be excused from paying dues. Technically, he is still a member, but he is not an active participant.

But some chapters will not permit a quiet dissociation, and the student is bound morally, if not legally, into active membership by being required to pay dues or to live in the fraternity house. Some Greek houses even impose fines or other penalties for nonparticipation. This is more common among chapters whose membership strength is below par.

Wrong choice? Too bad

Most national social fraternities insist—as a prerequisite to initiation—that the candidate promise never to join another college social fraternity. And national college fraternities usually respect each others' rules. Suppose, for example, that a student was a member of a particular national fraternity on one campus and then transferred to another college, where he joined a different social fraternity. If either organization ever learned of the dual membership, the student probably would be unceremoniously expelled from both.

This frowning upon dual membership, of course, applies only to the national fraternities, and does not relate to the professional, honorary, or service fraternities or societies.

Membership in a social fraternity does not preclude membership in these other types of Greek-letter fraternal organizations, nor does it prevent students from joining other college clubs. Indeed, most fraternities and sororities encourage members to affiliate with other campus groups.

But most graduates who have been members say that fraternity life forms the hub of their outside social activity.

Students who are members of fraternal organizations— or any other campus activities, for that matter—find it's quite easy to get very involved in their associations. This is especially true for officers or committee heads. Individuals often feel a great degree of loyalty to an organization and

receive inspiration from it. But the major goal in college—
that of getting a degree—should not be overlooked or set
aside for any length of time. Three or five years hence, the
degree will mean more to a student than any campus social
or fraternal ties. The degree, after all, is the meal ticket.

CHAPTER **19**

What Professionals Say

Publishers are naturally skeptical when they eye a manuscript —particularly an unusual one from an unknown author. Barron's is no exception. When the editors at Barron's read the manuscript, they said, "This is very sound advice you offer. But what do educators say about getting better grades?"

The author presented the manuscript to a noted husband and wife team of college professors who were asked to add their own comments—to write a chapter representing the college professors' point of view.

The author was a little skeptical himself at first. After all, this book basically represents the views of recent college graduates who took a few pot shots at some of the professionals and their stifled, traditional viewpoints. But not all college professionals sit in ivory towers. Indeed, some are quite down-to-earth and their ideas are not so different from our own.

Professors James and Marilyn Blawie were asked to write a chapter representing the professional educator's viewpoint. Both are highly respected educators with miles of learning and teaching behind them.

Professor James Blawie, B.A., A.M., J.D. and Ph.D. is professor of law at the University of Santa Clara and holds several academic honors. He taught political science, economics and business law at Columbia University and, with his wife Marilyn, co-authored two books.

Blawie is a reserve captain in the Army Judge Advocate General, reads and writes several languages, and is a member of the California and Connecticut Bar associations, as well as several specialized and federal Bar associations. He is listed in *Who's Who in the West.*

His wife, Marilyn, holds a B.A. and J.D. and is a professor of political science in the California State College system. She currently teaches at the California State College in Hayward, California. Mrs. Blawie was graduated with distinction and high honors from the University of Connecticut and studied at the University of Lund, in Sweden, and at the London School of Economics. She studied under two grants. Under another scholarship, she received a law degree from the University of Chicago. She has an extensive background as a professional writer of scholarly works and was associate editor of the state constitutional law project at Columbia University.

The mother of three children, Mrs. Blawie was elected to the governing board of a large junior college system in California and assisted in the development of a campus and curriculum. She is listed in *Who's Who Among American Women.*

Professional Educators Speak

By Professors Marilyn and James Blawie

The author has put down in these pages the kind of advice we wish we had been given when we were undergraduates. Straight from the shoulder talk is a rare commodity these days. It is the kind of advice a level-headed professor would give to a hard-working student who came to him looking for help.

You should be interested in the qualities which any good professor expects to find in a student. Seek the things a professor looks for in a student and on finding them, adopt them. If it acts like a good student, looks like a good student and talks like a good student, the professor will naturally assume that it *is* a good student.

First of all, let's clear up one point. Nobody really taught Mozart to play the fiddle, Armstrong the trumpet, Einstein mathematics, or the Blue Angels to fly. People like this break the mold, and there are no rules for them to follow. The same goes for people who just don't fit the academic mold because their minds run in other and maybe deeper channels. Edison and George Patton were lousy students, but they wore and wore and wore. If you're like this, throw this book away.

Discipline—a coordinating factor

So, genius aside, what are the signs of the superior student? First of all, discipline. Not snap to, brown nose discipline, but rather a quiet confidence, an ability to allocate time, a knowledge of personal good and bad points, abilities and limitations. To put it in another way, discipline is the internal ability to run your life so that you can do what you're expected to do when you're expected to do it.

This is the one factor which marks the good student more than any other. All professors love, fear and respect clean, cold intelligence in a student. But intelligence alone is worthless. In every group of college drop-outs, more are in the group because of a lack of self-discipline than because of a lack of ability or intelligence.

Motivation—the drive

In fact, most college professors will tell you that a strong back is more important than a strong mind for undergrads, and this even goes for graduate schools also. A person with 100 or 110 I.Q. who knows what he wants and is willing to do what is necessary to get it, will succeed if he is prepared to sweat enough and do what he has to do. If the author of this book had a dollar for every Ed.D., Ph.D., doctor and lawyer walking around with 110 I.Q. or less, he would be wealthy.

Know thyself

These people made the grade because they were smart enough to know their own abilities and limitations and to work within them. The same goes for you, and this is the very valuable lesson which these pages teach you. You learn to use the tools you have, you try to use them most favorably to yourself and to control as much as you can the occasions on which you have to use them.

Be willing to learn, adjust

Almost as important as discipline is mental flexibility, the open mind, the willingness and ability to think clearly, to weigh all sides of every question. You can say it in a lot of different ways, but what it means is that you attack a problem with your mind prepared to consider all possibilities, to probe to the heart, undeterred by preconceived notions.

This doesn't mean that you should just chuck your moral training or check your other beliefs at the door. But it does mean that you don't start out with any unproven propositions which relate to the problem. You play the academic game by being willing to listen, to speculate and to be convinced if the pattern which emerges is logical and fits what you know already.

What is different or unfamiliar is not necessarily better or worse. In fact, even the words *better* or *worse* indicate a judgment better left unmade at first. Your courses in philosophy, history, literature, sociology are likely to leave you a little unhappy, unsettled and unsure. But that is what they are supposed to do and what they have to do if you are to learn to think and to influence the world around you.

The old question, "Is it better to be a contented peasant or a discontented Socrates?" gets the point across pretty well. The good student realizes that he goes to college not to learn just a new skill like horseback riding. He goes to learn how to think and what to think about. You can't go home again, Tom Wolfe observed, and this refers to any college student, even the one who leaves college along the way. You will be a different person, the world will be smaller, your home town will look seedier and the people in it a little more limited. Be prepared for this change, because even an engineering student, home ec major or ag student undergoes it as part of the educational process.

The open mind, then, and a willingness to test and retest what you already know or believe, marks the good student. Other times, other arts, other cultures, other customs, other beliefs, other sciences and other techniques—all are part of the process you have to undergo to get that degree. Go along willingly.

The art of communicating

You may have heard this elsewhere, but the ability to talk and to write clearly is very important to college success. The author has concentrated, rightly, on the ability to read well and to learn and remember what you read. You are judged in a good many courses, however, by what you say and what you write. And it isn't just lit majors, journalists and history students we are talking about. It is every student.

Perhaps you have been told that writing isn't really important anymore, or that you don't have to worry about spelling or grammar because every businessman, scientist, geologist and so on has a competent secretary to take care of that stuff. Nonsense. You have to be able to write well enough to communicate your ideas with some ability to qualify and shade meaning. You also have to be able to talk well enough so that you don't sound like the village idiot.

This doesn't mean that you have to write really well. College professors long ago gave up hoping for the unbelievable class in which most students would be able to spell correctly, punctuate in the right places, avoid dangling participles and split infinitives and know when to end a sentence. But it does mean that you have to be able to write well enough so that your sentences mean what you think they mean, and not two other things instead or as well. You rarely get the benefit of the doubt in such cases, even from indulgent professors.

To sum up this point, it is wonderful if you have a charming literary style, or if you write a clean, spare American journalese. However, most students don't and you don't have to be this proficient. What you do have to write, however, is a fairly clear, unambiguous style with a minimum of spelling and gross grammatical errors. If you can't do this, take steps to correct things before you wash out.

Don't be afraid to sign up for bonehead English courses or for similar courses artfully disguised under such titles as An Introduction to Modern American Prose Style—to which an advisor or professor may direct you. Even better, try to do something about it before you enter college, or before you start your second year if you barely manage to survive the first year.

Most public school systems, YMCA's and YMHA's, public

libraries and similar groups offer remedial writing, speaking and reading courses. Take advantage of them—this is all part of that discipline mentioned earlier. Know where you're short and do something about it.

Another good technique is to take a foreign language course, either at college as an auditor, for no credit, or in one of the facilities mentioned above. Try something like German or Russian or French, so that you will have to think a little bit about your own language to make headway in the new language. There's an old saying that the best way to learn to use your own language is to study another one. Also—say you study German nights during the summer and just scrape through the Y course. You can drop it there, or take the same course again at college in the fall, giving you a repeat of the same material, more language training and a fairly easy grade in a "scholarly" subject.

Forget the speech courses. You've spoken the language since you were two or three. Make a real effort to think about what you're saying, to cut out some of the rough slang, to talk in short, complete sentences and to make what you say clear without using hand gestures or other aids. Probably the most important thing is to make your sentences short and drop out words and phrases like "really," "you know what I mean" and other meaningless bridges. Better to shut your mouth and think of what you are going to say next. And talk the right way all the time, not just in class.

We're willing to help you

There is no doubt that a professor is impressed by a student who talks in short, direct sentences and writes the same way, even if a little polish is missing here and there.

Now for some specifics. The author's suggestion that students make use of a professor's office hours is well put. Most instructors are happy to talk with students almost any time when other duties don't interfere, so don't be afraid to drop in at any convenient time. All he can do is tell you that he's busy and suggest another time.

Even more important, though, in our computer age, is for the professor to get some impression of you for the future. You'd be surprised at the number of students who look around for a few references just before or after graduation and can't find even one instructor who really knows or remembers them.

Don't drop in and ask him to repeat a lecture which you missed for no particularly good reason, or for some easy tutoring which you could get as well yourself from your texts or from a trip to the library. Do drop in if you are particularly interested in part of the course and want to get some insight on it from a man who knows a lot about it. Drop in also if you have personal problems which affect your course performance or if you have a genuine difficulty with the subject— one which hangs on after an honest effort to resolve it for yourself.

There is another reason for getting to know the instructor. You would be surprised at the number of requests professors get for information about a particular student. Often a professor draws a complete blank when told that John Andrews was in his class two years ago and gave him as a reference. If the inquirer is from the personnel section of a prospective employer or is an FBI or military intelligence man doing an agency check in the course of clearing your records for government contract work or a commission, this does you no good at all. However, it is better than having the instructor ponder for a minute, then answer, "Oh, that idiot." So get to know your prof, but make a good impression.

The professor normally has more things to do than time to do them in, so don't be put off by an initial cold reaction. The prof probably wishes you'd just go away and let him take care of the work that is already two weeks behind. But stay there. In a few minutes, he will be trying to help you and will usually even lose track of time.

Look at the prof, not his tests

There's an old saying among college students, "Take the man and not the course." This means simply that you shouldn't pass up the outstanding lecturer because you're afraid he will give hard exams. Chances are that taking his course will be one of the high points of your college life, and that you will do a lot better than you think. You really attend a lecture not merely for information, but for the instructor's mature insight into his subject and for his informed prejudice. It is an old truism that only a man who knows his subject inside out can explain it to an untrained audience in simple and easily understood terms.

Most good students finish college with one big regret: that they left without taking a course from a particular professor. The drive to get good grades is so great that the bad professor often drives the good one out of the marketplace. Take the course from the good professor, even if you hear he's hard. A lot of what you hear is put out by poor students or those with a grudge. If you know that a particular professor is outstanding, or that you like what he says, take the chance and sign up.

Closely related to this is the universal undergraduate custom of one student's asking another what courses and which instructors to take. There is some good in that approach, but use it with some common sense. The advice of a junior or senior with a solid academic record is worth seeking. The advice of a second year student who barely got through his freshman year is almost worthless. A lot of students will tell you that the best course or the best instructor they had in college was one they were forced to take because no other course was open, or because the instructor of their original choice was ill and unable to teach. So, while it pays to get some advice, use it with caution and sense.

Profs agree on the value of cramming

In talking about cramming, the author shows wisdom beyond his academic years. *No, and we repeat, no law student or doctoral candidate in any respectable academic field ever made it without day upon day and week upon week of cramming.* While we could never go along with an all-night cram the night before an exam, the three o'clock cram is an ancient and respected part of any good student's life. When the author says that it is better to be tired and informed than wide awake and ignorant, he has the proven testimony drawn from the experience of most doctors, lawyers and academicians.

An extra sentence

Also, in advising a student taking an exam to spend all the time available in rereading, recalculating, etc., the author is on the soundest ground. Any professor will tell you that what seems like mere repetition (or saying the same thing in another way) to a person who is very familiar with the subject often serves as additional and valuable information to one who is not so familiar with it. Every professor has had the experience of grading a paper and being totally disappointed with the answer up to the point where a student says "or to put it another way," or "to sum up" and then gives exactly the analysis the professor is looking for.

Don't keep writing if you don't know what you're writing about. But if you do know what you're saying, keep going. An old student maxim has it that "in length, there's strength," or more bitterly, "they don't read it, they weigh it." Don't write just for the sake of writing, but if you think that you can make the point clearer or add something to what you've written, *by all means do it*. Few instructors mark off for length unless they specify a certain length in advance.

Other things that add up

The author does an excellent job of recommending ways to make study easier, but only briefly mentions one of the most familiar ones. You probably know already that certain fields are best studied by intensive reading of the text, as in mathematics, accounting, zoology and the like. However, college courses in fields like history, art criticism, philosophy, social psychology or international relations are often best studied by going beyond the text. In fact, a single careful reading of the text will give you most of what's in it, so rather than rereading it, you are better off reading a similar text by a different author. In such fields, a great deal depends on point of view or the school of interpretation to which the author belongs. This means that reading another collateral text opens up new avenues and new insights which can't help but impress the instructor in class discussion or in exams. Be sure of one thing, though, and that is that you actually *read* the text to which you refer. The instructor is usually happy to recommend another good text covering the course material. An upperclass student majoring in the field is also a good source of advice on a collateral text. You can learn half again or twice as much about such a subject by reading two different texts carefully rather than by reading one text twice.

Sound advice on term papers has been given by the author, and here is a little tip which may make the actual composition easier. Instructors will usually allow a student to group all his footnotes on a separate page or pages at the end of the paper if he clears the matter in advance. Manuscripts for publication in scholarly journals are prepared in this way, so the instructor will be familiar with the style. He will usually permit it unless he is trying specifically to teach a particular form.

One point which the author fails to raise is the *desirability* of sitting up front in class. One of us was a determined back-of-the-room sitter like most students, and the other sat up front or in back depending on whether the course was interesting or not. We both now agree that the nitwits naturally gravitate to the back and the good students to the front. They do this for a very practical reason. You can't goof off without attracting attention when you sit up front. Any student who has tried both will tell you that he learned more when he sat up front, because he had to stay awake and pay attention. It is sound advice to sit up front and to attend every class, even if you do feel exposed and don't get to horse around with the opposite sex so easily on the firing line.

One student who took a two-semester course remarked that he had found the first semester, when he sat in back of a large class, dull and uninteresting. The second semester, with fewer classmates, he decided to sit up front. He reported that he found that the instructor had qualities he had never appreciated before, and that the course material seemed much more interesting. The student was bright enough to figure out that things fit together better when he paid attention, and that the course had not improved so much as his appreciation of it.

We want to hear from you

From time to time, some educational genius tries to throw a scare into us professors by threatening to replace us with television tapes of the "greats" in our field. Some of these geniuses have been amazed that professors do not take the threat seriously and even seem to act as if they haven't heard it at all. Why aren't profs afraid of automation?

It's simply because college classes are a two-way business. The professor has something to say and he wants the student to hear it. There is the occasional professor who thinks that this is all there is to it. He writes the draft of his obscure treatise on education in Macedonian Greece, and then reads it to class after class of students. But this professor is the exception, more European than American.

The average American professor teaches because he has something to say and because he likes the excitement and intellectual challenge of communicating new and disquieting ideas and facts to students in various stages of ignorance, confusion, rebellion, immaturity or learning. It is the rare professor who won't set aside his lecture to follow a thoughtful student's questions and comments.

The author has recommended attending classes regularly and participating in them. Acquaint yourself with at least two other members of the class, and attempt to talk things over with them outside of class. Don't shut your mind to the content of the course when you slam your notebook at end of class.

When you're in class, follow what the instructor is saying.

Do you disagree? Read enough so you know what he was driving at and what the experts in the field have to say. One of us recalls with satisfaction the student who took strong exception to an excerpt from an article about activities by racial minorities during the Great Depression. After taking the instructor to task for reading this item in class, he disappeared into the library. Absent from class for two weeks, he emerged admitting he was wrong, and with a bit more of that open mind we mentioned above. He went on to become a successful graduate student and professional despite his marginal first years in college. Later, he described this incident and a couple of similar ones as turning points in his career.

This kind of experience will not be possible in every course. One man's delight is another's despair. Choose your required general education courses carefully to minimize those which you don't like and would probably do poorly in. A social science student, for instance, might find it advisable to fill a science requirement by taking a course called the philosophy of science or conservation of natural resources rather than physics or chemistry.

It is a rare professor who will let any personal feeling about a student influence the grade which he gives. There are instructors who don't meet the ethical norm of the profession, just as there are in any field. But the ordinary professor will bend over backward to avoid showing favoritism or dislike. In fact, a student who particularly irritates his instructor will usually receive a determinedly cautious and impartial estimate of his performance. There are no rules to this sort of thing, and you play it by ear, just as in any other part of life. But don't give a professor presents or try to influence him indirectly by offering to hire him as a tutor or help him get a part-time research job. Then he very well may torpedo you.

Successful friends—successful you

The friends you find in college will also influence your success or lack of it. Wise is the C student who seeks out an A or B student instead of another C student or a D or F student. Ask that A or B student what he got out of the assigned reading or the lecture, or if he agrees with your analysis of a problem. If you're working on some sort of a group project, don't stick like grim death to a group of buddies who are doing no better than you in a course. Don't hang out with losers who moan about the textbook, the lecturer, and the college. The very thought of some of the study groups which the prof knows have been formed is enough to drive him to drink.

Though there are exceptions, most good students like to help classmates who are not making the grade. Good students like to talk and to teach. One's approach may provide them with new insight or an opportunity to try out their own half-formed ideas.

Become a part of college

The more time you can spend in and around college people and the more you can steep yourself in the college community, the greater your chance of success. If you like choir singing, join the college chorus or glee club "for the duration." See college art shows, hear concerts and attend special lectures. If any of the faculty members have "at home" nights, drop in. Hang around the college library, read the magazines and borrow good books. The old city library is just no good for college work. Be a college student in spirit as well as in name, and you'll find the whole process easier and more enjoyable.

When you go to college there are certain choices that you must make. More and more students are living home and commuting to classes. It seems that every third student who comes into a professor's office has a tale that goes something like this: He is having trouble attending his courses because he has a full-time job with frequent changes in shifts. In addition, he has a family made up of a non-working wife and three small children. Another variation from younger students concerns parents who insist that Sundays be reserved for visiting relatives, another day as family "at home day," and parents who insist on lights out at ten, study or no. Usually there is a car that needs maintenance and sports activities which absolutely must be spectated. These tales are especially prevalent around examination time or paper due date.

These students *just haven't committed themselves psychologically and by time allocation to college study*. The old saw about two to three hours in out-of-class work for every one at lecture still has a lot to it. But how about the forty-hour week? For college students there is no such animal unless the student is part time. A student with a full time job, heavy family and other obligations should reduce his commitments to a minimum and plan on a part time load.

A needy student should consider taking a low or no interest bank or student loan to help him through college as an alternative to keeping a full time job and reaping low grades. If the collar fits, find the loan and scholarship advisor and talk to him.

The type of job is important too. One of us counseled a student from a poor family. He never did much better than low C or high D work despite a grueling study schedule. Investigation showed that he was working nights stocking shelves in a closed supermarket. He worked alone and had no opportunity during these 40 hours to study, to talk or to advance himself in his college work. He was advised to try to find a job in the college library or one of the college offices. He was told that the pay might not be as good, but the opportunity to learn how colleges operate, to observe scholarly activity and to listen and to talk at a high level might make the difference. Some time later, he had reached the C level and for the first time did a good job on oral class reports. The federal government in its War on Poverty programs has recently recognized this problem and has provided funds for campus jobs for those in the low-income brackets. Inquire on campus if you think you qualify.

Some spare time activity should be directed to out-of-class education, particularly when the student is from a non-college family. Except for the physical education or recreation major, most college students will learn little from warming a sports spectator's seat week after week. There is much value in active sport and exercise. However, every student should read a good book or a serious magazine once in a while, or listen to the more serious offerings on radio or television. In an early manual for college-bound students, we observed that a good proportion of those who succeed in college frequently read one or more of the following: *The Saturday Review of Literature, The New York Times, Harper's, The Atlantic Monthly,* opinion magazines, and a good news magazine like *Newsweek.*

Anyone can graduate from college if he is good enough to be admitted in the first place. All it takes is *determination, discipline, and a strong back.*

The
eading
SAT Study Guide

evised Tenth Edition
amuel C. Brownstein and Mitchel Weiner
72 pp. $6.95 pa. $19.00 cl.
omplete preparation for the SAT,
SAT/NMSQT, ACT, and College Board
chievement Tests

Model Examinations: Practice your skills
nd preview your results. With sample
uestions that help you discover your weak
oots and develop your strengths.
cludes: VERBAL APTITUDE TEST
ATHEMATICAL APTITUDE TEST
EST OF STANDARD WRITTEN ENGLISH

elf-Instructional Study Plans: Specially
esigned study programs for the three parts of
e examination. These are systematic methods
f reviewing and improving your score.

ath Review: 950 practice questions on
rithmetic, fractions, decimals, percent,
eometry, coordinate geometry

erbal Review: 1000 questions on vocabulary /
25 sentence completion drills;
00 word relationship practice items/
75 reading comprehension questions

Grammar Refresher: The fundamentals of basic
English, as required by most colleges.
With practice exercises that strengthen
skills in grammar and usage.

Also: With typical CEEB Achievement Tests
in the following subjects:
English Composition
(including the new Essay Portion),
Math Level 1, Biology, Physics, Chemistry,
French, German, Spanish

Also available:

BASIC TIPS ON THE SAT
Brownstein & Weiner; pa., $2.95
Brief preparatory course for the SAT
with a model test; answers explained.

At your local bookseller or order direct adding
10% postage plus applicable sales tax.

BARRON'S

113 Crossways Park Drive, Woodbury, N.Y. 11797